BREAKFAST WITH THE ANGELS

Breakfast with the Angels

120 DAILY READINGS

COMPILED BY TRACI MULLINS

VINE
BOOKS

Servant Publications
Ann Arbor, Michigan

Vine Books is an imprint of Servant Publications especially designed to serve
evangelical Christians.

Published by Servant Publications
P.O. Box 8617
Ann Arbor, Michigan 48107

Cover design: Left Coast Design, Inc., Portland, Oregon
Cover and interior illustrations: Angels through the Ages, Planet Art.

The editor and publishers express their appreciation to the publishers listed at
the end of the book for permission to reprint the copyrighted selections. Every
effort has been made to trace all copyright owners; if any acknowledgment has
been inadvertently omitted, the publishers will gladly make the necessary correc-
tion in the next printing.

96 97 98 99 00   10 9 8 7 6 5 4 3 2 1

Printed in the United States of America
ISBN 0-89283-991-0

LIBRARY OF CONGRESS CATALOGING-IN-PUBLICATION DATA

Breakfast with the angels : 120 daily readings / compiled by Traci Mullins.
    p.   cm.
  Includes bibliographical references.
  ISBN 0-89283-991-0
  1. Angels—Meditations.   I. Mullins, Traci.
BT966.2.B69   1996
235'.3—dc20   96-21950
                                                                    CIP

❧❧❧❧❧❧

Not only does God love you,
but the angels love you, too.[1]

❧❧❧❧❧❧

1

Angels See God Fully

We can only imagine what it must be like to see God's face—to accurately perceive his beauty, his incredible power, his holiness, his love, and his majesty. Different ones of us vary in our capacity to see God, but none of us yet has the ability to know him as he knows us. It's as though God is telling us that it's still too dangerous. It would be like trying to pour Niagara Falls into a tiny thimble. The thimble would be utterly crushed and destroyed. This side of eternity, we are yet too full of distortions, sin, and frailty to look God in the eye.

Yet Jesus tells us that these angels continually enjoy this face-to-face communion with God. Maybe that's why they make such great guardians. They know how overwhelmingly attractive God really is, and they are not seduced, as we are, into making idols out of lesser desires. They see the foolishness of choosing anything less than God. The things that tempt us do not tempt them.[2]

In freely choosing to serve as the agents of divine purpose, angels are the living expression of the prayer "Thy will be done."[3]

2

What Is an Angel?

What *is* an angel? The two words that come closest to a true biblical answer are "manifestation" and "servant." Most of us know what a servant is, but what is a manifestation? Putting together several dictionary meanings we arrive at this definition: To manifest means to reveal, prove, display, and put beyond doubt the nature of that which is manifested. Since God and angels exist to manifest and serve him, then what angels do is to reveal, prove, and display God's love.

Angels carry the love of God where he wants it this day, this moment. And since the heavenly Father's love is limitless, another fact follows—angels may be found doing anything, any time, any place, any way to help God's people.[4]

∞

Angels are God's messengers whose chief business is to carry out his orders in the world. He has given them an ambassadorial charge. He has designated and empowered them as holy deputies to perform works of righteousness. In this way they assist him as their creator while he sovereignly controls the universe. So he has given them the capacity to bring his holy enterprises to a successful conclusion.[5]

Angels Will Win the Victory

The night before his trial, Peter, bound with chains, was sleeping between two soldiers, and "sentries stood guard at the entrance." In other words, his arrest was well-secured, and there wasn't a flicker of hope that he could escape.

Suddenly an angel appeared, lighting the cell. "Quick, get up!" he said, and as the chains fell off Peter's wrists, the angel added, "And you better get dressed." Lights came on. The angel was talking. Chains were clinking. Peter was shuffling around getting dressed. Yet the guards kept snoring! This was the other half of the miracle.

Still trying to blink the sleep out of his eyes, Peter followed the angel out of the prison. Passing by two other guards and watching the prison gate swing open of its own accord, Peter found himself standing in the dark street outside the prison.[6]

Spiritual forces and resources are available to all Christians. Because our resources are unlimited, Christians will be winners. Millions of angels are at God's command and at our service. The hosts of heaven stand at attention as we make our way from earth to glory, and Satan's BB guns are no match for God's heavy artillery. So don't be afraid. God is for you. He has committed his angels to wage war in the conflict of the ages—and they will win the victory.[7]

4

The Fiery Furnace

You have issued a decree, O king, that everyone who hears the sound of music must fall down and worship the image of gold, and that whoever does not fall down and worship will be thrown into a blazing furnace. But there are some Jews—Shadrach, Meshach, and Abednego—who pay no attention to you. They neither serve your gods nor worship the image of gold you have set up."

Furious with rage, Nebuchadnezzar summoned Shadrach, Meshach, and Abednego, and said to them, "Is it true that you do not serve my gods or worship the image I have set up? Now when you hear the sound of music, if you are ready to fall down and worship the image I made, very good. But if you do not worship it, you will be thrown immediately into a blazing furnace. Then what god will be able to rescue you from my hand?"

Shadrach, Meshach, and Abednego replied to the king, "O Nebuchadnezzar, we do not need to defend ourselves before you in this matter. If we are thrown into the blazing furnace, the God we serve is able to save us from it, and he will rescue us from your hand. But even if he does not, we will not serve your gods or worship the image of gold you have set up."

Then Nebuchadnezzar was furious. He ordered the furnace heated seven times hotter than usual and commanded some of the strongest soldiers in his army to tie up Shadrach, Meshach, and Abednego and throw them into the blazing furnace. The furnace was so hot that the flames of the fire killed the soldiers who took up Shadrach, Meshach, and Abednego, and these three men, firmly tied, fell into the blazing furnace.

Then King Nebuchadnezzar leaped to his feet in amazement and asked his advisers, "Weren't there three men that we tied up and threw into the fire?"

They replied, "Certainly, O king."

He said, "Look! I see four men walking around in the fire, unbound and unharmed, and the fourth looks like a son of the gods."

Then Nebuchadnezzar said, "Praise be to the God of Shadrach, Meshach, and Abednego, who has sent his angel and rescued his servants!"[8]

5

Angels: Fellow Citizens

Whoever doesn't believe in angels doesn't believe in the Scriptures. Jesus himself spoke many times of angels. Why shouldn't God have created angels, those great, invisible intelligences full of light? Are we going to doubt their existence simply because we can't see them?

Angels are said to "carry" our prayers to God (a kind of figurative way of speaking, like the expression, "I carry the people I love in my heart"), which shows how all of creation is beautifully bound together: men and angels in Christ, in God.

In this unity, angels are said to be "messengers" between God and men, ascending with our prayers and descending with graces.

Angels take an interest in men. Jesus said that the angels rejoice when one sinner repents. They have been called our "fellow-citizens." We all have something to do with one another—God doesn't create in separate compartments. We are all in life together.[9]

∞

Angels are spiritual beings, superior in nature to man, who were created by God to serve him obediently and to act as his messengers to us. Angels are more popular among us than are saints and appear in the plots of our motion pictures with regularity. Possibly their ecumenical character has something to do with their eternal appeal; all religions have angels or their analog, and the best-known angels, Gabriel, Raphael, and Michael, are called by name in the three monotheistic religions.[10]

6

Why Should We Care About Angels?

The Bible is an excellent resource book from which to learn about angels. The Old Testament alone refers to angels 108 times. The New Testament, which is much shorter than the Old Testament, nevertheless speaks of angels even more often—165 times.

You can't believe in the God revealed in the Bible without believing also in angels.[11]

∞

Like it or not, angels are important players in the drama of salvation. Isn't it time we paid a little more attention to these powerful and loving allies that God has given us? True, there are dangers. We must never forget that worship belongs only to God, no matter how beautiful or powerful some of his creatures may be. We must also remember that angels are but one way that God works in the universe. Pascal said, "We create angels, but trouble comes if we create too many." They aren't the whole story, nor even the most important part of the story. They are simply supporting actors, servants of the living God, as we are. Even so, such fears fail to justify our ignorance of the angels. Knowing more about their nature and purpose will help us to perceive more of God's own majesty and his loving plan for our lives.... If we let them, angels can be a window to God, offering a glimpse of his power, his goodness, and his loving intentions toward us.[12]

7

The Fourth Man

It had been reckless of me, taking a before-dawn stroll through the tangle of streets behind the Los Angeles bus terminal. But I was a young woman arriving in the great city for the first time. My job interview was five hours away, and I couldn't wait to explore!

Now I'd lost my way in a Skid Row neighborhood. I saw three men lurking behind me, trying to keep out of sight in the shadows. Trembling with fright, I did what I always do when in need of help. I bowed my head and asked God to rescue me.

But when I looked up, a fourth man was striding toward me in the dark! *Dear God, I'm surrounded.* I was so scared, it took me a few seconds to realize that even in the blackness I could *see* this man. He was dressed in an immaculate workshirt and denim pants, and carried a lunchbox. His face was stern but beautiful (the only word for it).

I ran up to him. "I'm lost and some men are following me," I said in desperation.

"Come," he said. "I'll take you to safety."

"I don't know what would have happened if you hadn't come along."

"I do." His voice was resonant, deep.

"I prayed for help just before you came."

A smile touched his mouth and eyes. We were nearing the depot. "You are safe now. Good-bye, Euphie."

Going into the lobby, it hit me. *Euphie!* Had he really used my first name? I whirled, burst out onto the sidewalk. But he had vanished.[13]

8

A Woodworking Angel

In Santa Fe, New Mexico, the Sisters of Loretto maintain an old adobe mission chapel, famous even today for its unusual staircase.

A brilliant European architect designed the interior of the chapel for the sisters. But its construction was well underway in 1878 when someone made a horrifying discovery: the plans included a high choir loft overlooking the chapel from the rear, but no staircase with which to reach it—and no room whatsoever to squeeze one in!

The sisters sent out an urgent plea for designer-carpenters. "Please, please come. The one who can solve our problem will be paid well to build the stairs...." Many men came. No one could do it. The sisters, in despair, prayed.

One day a quiet man arrived with a load of lumber on his burro. Somehow, he obtained adequate authorization to proceed with his attempt to build the staircase. Day after day, he labored steadily from the floor up, building an elegant spiral staircase with an unfamiliar type of wood. He seemed to have no written plans. He used only wooden pegs to fasten the pieces together, and his work was expertly precise. He built thirty-three narrow but sturdy steps with no central support and no banister. They were beautiful! Who was this itinerant genius?

Loading his burro with his meager toolkit and even more meager personal possessions, the ordinary-looking fellow simply left town, never accepting any payment, never to be seen again.[14]

9

The Angel in the Storm

The ship was caught by the storm and could not head into the wind; so we gave way to it and were driven along. As we passed to the lee of a small island called Cauda, we were hardly able to make the lifeboat secure. When the men had hoisted it aboard, they passed ropes under the ship itself to hold it together. We took such a violent battering from the storm that the next day they began to throw the cargo overboard. When neither sun nor stars appeared for many days and the storm continued raging, we finally gave up all hope of being saved.

After the men had gone a long time without food, Paul stood up before them and said: "Men, you should have taken my advice not to sail from Crete; then you would have spared yourselves this damage and loss. But now I urge you to keep up your courage, because not one of you will be lost; only the ship will be destroyed. Last night an angel of the God whose I am and whom I serve stood beside me and said, 'Do not be afraid, Paul. You must stand trial before Caesar; and God has graciously given you the lives of all who sail with you.' So keep up your courage, men, for I have faith in God that it will happen just as he told me."[15]

10

The Ethereal Rescuer

Dr. L. Larson, a retired clergyman from Moorhead, Minnesota, spoke of the time when two sisters, aged eight and four, fell into a river near the church where he had his parish ministry.

While the hysterical mother screamed that her daughters could not swim, a man who had been fishing from a boat set out at once on a rescue attempt. Although the fisherman was determined to make a valiant effort, in his heart he felt that there would be no way that he could reach the little girls before they drowned. He truly feared that his efforts would be futile.

When he pulled alongside them, however, he found the little girls floating calmly in an "unnatural manner," as if they were "somehow supported from underneath."

Dr. Larson said that men and women who had watched the rescue from the shore stated that they had seen a beautiful person in white supporting the girls until the fisherman overtook them. The girls themselves insisted that an angel had prevented them from sinking under the water, and they described their ethereal rescuer in vivid detail.[16]

∞

"See that you do not look down on one of these little ones. For I tell you that their angels in heaven always see the face of my Father in heaven."[17]

The Wonderful Friendship of Angels

The angels are part of God's ingenious provision for us. Because they are so passionately in love with God, the angels are perfectly conformed to his will. Whatever he tells them to do they do. Whoever he loves, they can't help but love. Because God cares for us so deeply, we can claim the wonderful friendship of angels.

What a tremendous encouragement to know that we are surrounded on every side by loving and powerful protectors. Thinking of angels can ease our sorrows, strengthen our faith, and lighten our hearts. G. K. Chesterton once quipped that "the angels can fly because they take themselves lightly." Of course the angels take themselves lightly. They keep things in perspective in a way that we can't. After all, they live in the presence of God himself. Their vision is clear, unclouded by the confusion and doubts we suffer. Neither do they fall prey to the insidious sin of pride, which weighs us down and chains us to our own small vision of the world. As we learn more about angels and their service, we will learn more about God. Our appetite for the spiritual life will increase and our longing for intimacy with our Creator will grow.[18]

12

Sublime Creatures

There is a kind of sublime creature which cleaves to the true and truly eternal God with so chaste a love that it is never detached from him nor does it flow away from him into any variety and vicissitude of time, but rests in the true and perfect contemplation of him alone.

And this is because you, God, show yourself to him who loves you as much as you command, and you are sufficient to him, so that he never falls away from you nor declines toward self.

O happy creature, if such a creature there is! Happy in clinging to your blessed happiness, happy in you, its eternal inhabitant and enlightener![19]

∞

All testify that the society of angels is virtually a perfect one in itself. No dissension, no jealousy, no burning ambition, no violence mar its surface. No one is preferred, no one left out. All know their gifts and abilities and responsibilities, and all work ceaselessly to perfect them and to be faithful to their duties. All have unlimited scope for growth, and all have "hearts" immovably fixed upon God. The only law is the law of love.[20]

∞

Angelic beings have a free will—just as we have—but one that—unlike ours—is totally focused on the will of God. This is the reason for their unbridled joy. They have found the secret of true contentment: *thinking of and concentrating on God rather than themselves.*[21]

13

Angels Become Dim Next to the God They Worship

A proper understanding of angels will never interfere with our heartfelt relationship with Jesus, but is much more likely to enhance it. It will give us a much deeper appreciation of his rightful position in that vast spiritual realm that we take now merely on faith. Paul summarized it beautifully:

> Christ is the visible likeness of the invisible God. He is the first-born son, superior to all created things. For through him God created everything in heaven and on earth, the seen and the unseen things, including spiritual powers, lords, rulers, and authorities.　COLOSSIANS 1:15-16

No matter where or when angels appear, no matter why they have been sent, their objective is to glorify the God-Man who died a bloody death on the cross for our sake. They do this by adoring him and instantly obeying God's command in our regard, for Jesus is indeed the King of angels![22]

∞

As glorious as the angelic and heavenly beings are, they become dim beside the inexpressible glory resident in our heavenly Lamb, the Lord of glory, to whom all powers in heaven and on earth bow in holy worship and breathless adoration.[23]

Holy, Holy, Holy

From the throne came flashes of lightning, rumblings, and peals of thunder. Before the throne, seven lamps were blazing. These are the seven spirits of God. Also before the throne there was what looked like a sea of glass, clear as crystal.

In the center, around the throne, were four living creatures, and they were covered with eyes, in front and in back. The first living creature was like a lion, the second was like an ox, the third had a face like a man, the fourth was like a flying eagle. Each of the four living creatures had six wings and was covered with eyes all around, even under his wings. Day and night they never stop saying: "Holy, holy, holy is the Lord God Almighty, who was, and is, and is to come." Whenever the living creatures give glory, honor, and thanks to him who sits on the throne and who lives for ever and ever, the twenty-four elders fall down before him who sits on the throne, and worship him who lives for ever and ever. They lay their crowns before the throne and say: "You are worthy, our Lord and God, to receive glory and honor and power, for you created all things, and by your will they were created and have their being."[24]

15

A Wing's Caress

Suddenly, a voice called out: "You there,
you three alone, what occupies your mind?"
I gave a start like some shy beast in panic.

I raised my head to see who just now spoke;
and never in a furnace was there seen
metal or glass so radiantly red

as was the being who said to me: "If you
are looking for the way to climb, turn here:
here is the path for those who search for peace."

Though blinded by the brilliance of his look,
I turned around and groped behind my guides,
letting the words just heard direct my feet.

Soft as the early morning breeze of May,
which heralds dawn, rich with the grass and flowers,
spreading in waves their breathing fragrances,

I felt a breeze strike soft upon my brow:
I felt a wing caress it, I am sure,
I sensed the sweetness of ambrosia.

I heard the words: "Blessed are those in whom
grace shines so copiously that love of food
does not arouse excessive appetite,

but lets them hunger after righteousness."[25]

16

Angels Don't Want Our Worship

I, John, am the one who heard and saw these things. And when I had heard and seen them, I fell down to worship at the feet of the angel who had been showing them to me. But he said to me, "Do not do it! I am a fellow servant with you and with your brothers the prophets and of all who keep the words of this book. Worship God!"[26]

∞

The souls of the blessed immortals who inhabit heaven have no nature superior to themselves save God, the Creator of the world and the soul itself, and these heavenly spirits derive their blessed life, and the light of truth, from the same source as ourselves, agreeing with the gGospel where we read, "There was a man sent from God whose name was John; the same came for a witness to bear witness of that Light, that through him all might believe. He was not that Light, but that he might bear witness of the Light. That was the true Light which lighteth every man that cometh into the world."[27]

∞

If any immortal power, no matter with what virtue endowed, loves us as himself, he must desire that we find our happiness by submitting ourselves to him, in submission to whom he himself finds happiness. If he does not worship God, he is wretched, because deprived of God; if he worships God, he cannot wish to be worshipped in God's stead. On the contrary, these higher powers acquiesce heartily in the divine sentence in which it is written, "He that sacrificeth unto any god, save unto the Lord only, he shall be utterly destroyed."[28]

17

Angels Are God's Agents in the Field

When my brother was missing in action during World War II, the mail carrier in our small town grieved with us as all our packages were returned, stamped "Deceased." But on the day a postcard arrived with Joe's signature—and assurance of his liberation from a German concentration camp—our mailman ran up our walk waving the postcard in jubilation! He shared our joy.

So, too, with our angels. They rejoice when we are freed from the prisons of unrepentant sin, of inordinate self-concern, or of cultural idolatry. The joy of angels escalates when we become radical followers of Christ, allowing ourselves to be completely led by the Spirit, as they themselves are led and empowered.[29]

∞

Angelic assistance is a part of God's universal plan of salvation. The *means* of salvation is the death and resurrection of Jesus Christ himself. Angels, however, are like God's agents in the field. He purposely uses them to introduce images, tendencies, and desires that lead us to do what is right and good.

For the most part, the spiritual guidance of angels is so unobtrusive as to go undetected. They will *never* compromise our free will. We are never forced to follow that which would be spiritually beneficial for us. Even so, this does not dim angels' desire to share with human beings the same immense ocean of love and joy that they themselves enjoy. This is the goal toward which they are constantly trying to maneuver and guide us.[30]

18

Angelic Love Points Us to God

Whoever these immortal and blessed inhabitants of heaven be, if they do not love us and wish us to be blessed, then we ought not to worship them; and if they do love us and desire our happiness, they cannot wish us to be made happy by any other means than they themselves have enjoyed—for how could they wish our blessedness to flow from one source, theirs from another?[31]

∞

Angel voices, ever singing
Round Thy throne of light;
Angel harps, forever ringing,
Rest not day or night.
Thousands only live to bless Thee,
And confess Thee,
Lord of Might.[32]

∞

The angels get excited whenever men and women begin to face the truth about themselves. They know that ever since Adam and Eve, we have been playing hide-and-seek with God and with each other, afraid to face the darkness in our own hearts and unwilling to admit our desperate need for God's forgiveness. Because the angels love us, they want to see us reconciled to the source of all joy, to God himself.[33]

19

The Angel Doll

Bonnie drove into the supermarket parking lot, her four-year-old daughter next to her, when suddenly she had a cerebral hemorrhage. For three weeks Bonnie lay comatose in a hospital bed, totally helpless and unresponsive.

"It was unbelievable after that, when I started coming around," she says. "The doctors. The nurses. My husband. Everyone pushing and prodding me to move, to talk, to do better, to try harder. Sometimes my head felt like it would explode.

"I begged God to give me some peace. I really needed peace inside. And then, almost in a flash, there seemed to be a large hand before me. On the palm, in block letters, my name was clearly spelled out. Right after, it was as though a steamroller was lifted from my chest. I felt so light. So peaceful.

"Then my eyes drifted to a small angel doll that someone had taped to my headboard. And it was like God telling me to look to my angel whenever I needed peace and comfort."

From then on, Bonnie's physical condition gradually began to improve. Through all the grueling therapy and learning to cope with residual handicaps, her faith and hope deepened to the point where she has a joy-filled ministry to other stroke victims.[34]

20

The Angel's Healing Kiss

Raymond Blomker and his wife had been told by several doctors that their seven-year-old daughter, Rebekah, would not recover from her lengthy illness. Each time the child began to speak of Christmas and the gifts that she most wanted, Blomker's heart felt as if it were being wrenched from his chest.

One night in October, as Blomker and his wife were praying for a miracle of healing at their sleeping daughter's bedside, they were distracted by the sound of a soft tapping on the windowpane.

To their astonishment, they saw a glowing light—which further startled them by moving through the closed window and materializing into an angel within Rebekah's bedroom. The being walked over to the sleeping child, bent to place a gentle kiss on her cheek, then disappeared.

Within moments Rebekah opened her eyes sleepily and smiled. "Can I get up and play now?" she asked, stifling a yawn. "My angel was just here and made me all better."

The next day the doctors confirmed that the Blomkers had received their miracle. Rebekah would live to see that Christmas—and many, many more.[35]

21

Angels in Times of Trouble

Some say, "If we have guardian angels, why don't we see them?" Maybe, without realizing it, we *have* seen our angels once or twice, or have heard them speak to us. Perhaps we are just blind and deaf to the unexpected. But our eyes and ears seem to open wide when we are in desperate straits, at least to judge by the number of accounts people give of angelic intervention in an emergency.

Karen Martin and her husband had purchased a brand-new truck and were going to pick it up. Karen was driving her minivan, and her husband, Don, was in the passenger seat when they stopped at a red light at the corner. To Karen's horror, she looked up to find a large station wagon turning from the far right lane and heading for her van, head-on, at forty-five miles per hour. There was no way the Martins could move.

Just before impact, Karen saw a strange sight—"Someone," in white light, was standing in front of her van. The white silhouette vanished as the two vehicles collided.

Although the collision was head-on and the station wagon was totaled, there were no injuries in either car—and the Martins' minivan needed no repairs other than a new bumper!

Karen says, "The only way I can explain what happened is the presence of a guardian angel."[36]

22

Angels Watchin' Over Us

All night, all day,
Angels watchin' over me, my Lord!
All night, all day,
Angels watchin' over me.

Now I lay me down to sleep,
Angels watchin' over me, my Lord!
Pray the Lord my soul to keep,
Angels watchin' over me.[37]

∞

The leaders of the Protestant reformation, who tended to down-play the often-sensationalized aspects of late medieval Christian faith, nevertheless agreed that angels had a role in everyday spiritual life. Martin Luther said, "[Angels act as] the Lord's soldiers, guardians, leaders, and protectors to preserve the creatures which he had created."[38]

23

"Cause Thy Angels to Surround Me..."

Corrie ten Boom writes of a remarkable experience at the Nazi Ravensbruck prison camp:

"Together we entered the building where there were women who took away all our possessions. Everyone had to undress completely.

"I asked if I might use the toilet. Betsie stayed close beside me all the time. Suddenly I had an inspiration, 'Quick, take off your woolen underwear,' I whispered to her. I rolled it up with mine and laid the bundle in a corner with my little Bible. 'The Lord is busy answering our prayers, Betsie,' I whispered.

"After we had had our showers and put on our shabby dresses, I hid the roll of underwear and my Bible under my dress. It did bulge out obviously; but I prayed, 'Lord, cause now thine angels to surround me; and let them not be transparent today, for the guards must not see me.' I felt perfectly at ease. Calmly I passed the guards. Everyone was checked, from the front, the sides, the back. The woman just in front of me had hidden a woolen vest under her dress; it was taken from her. They let me pass, for they did not see me. Betsie, right behind me, was searched.

"On each side of the door leading outside were women who felt everyone over for a second time. I knew they would not see me, for the angels were still surrounding me. I was not even surprised when they passed me by; but within me rose the jubilant cry, 'O Lord, if thou dost so answer prayer, I can face even Ravensbruck unafraid!'"[39]

24

Golden Weapons

A pediatric nurse and member of an evangelical sisterhood was serving in Danzig in 1945 after Russian troops had overrun many German towns. Local women were being abused, and nights were filled with terror. Nurses gathered as many women and children as they could and found temporary lodging in a small makeshift school. The people called their building "the island of peace," because nothing bad ever seemed to happen there.

One day a woman brought her children and begged the nurses to take them. The children had had a completely secular upbringing and had never seen anyone pray. That evening, as the community held a worship service, the new boy, instead of folding his hands with the rest, stared into the distance with wide eyes. The community sang a familiar song, asking God to send angels to "place golden weapons around our beds."

"When we said Amen, the boy came up to me and drew me out of the building," the nurse reported. "He kept tapping his breastbone and saying, 'Up to here. It came up to here on them.'"

The nurse asked him what he meant. Pointing to the gutter on the roof of the building, he repeated his statement. "The gutter came up to here on them!"

"What are you talking about?" the nurse asked.

The child told her that while everyone had been singing, he had seen a man ablaze with light at every corner of the building. The men were so tall that they towered above the roof.[40]

25

Strange Lights

Sometime around 1950, missionaries named Egbert and Hattie Dyk went to work at Tseltal, an Indian village near Santo Domingo [Dominican Republic]. All but one resident eventually became Christians, but since there was much persecution from neighbors, the entire village packed up, walked for a day, and established a Christian community in the new place.

It seems that a man named Domingo Hernandez lived near this area and hated his Christian neighbors. He was determined to burn their settlement and slaughter all its inhabitants. Late one night he organized his fellow villagers, prepared pitch-pine torches and canoes, and led them stealthily down the hill and across the river.

But before they had a chance to attack, they saw a bright light shining through the windows of every home in the Christian village. Then a strange luster shone over the entire area.

Domingo Hernandez and his men were so frightened that they turned and scrambled down the hill, plunged into the river, swam across, and ran, soaking wet, the half-mile to their homes.

The next morning, as the women from Hernandez's village were washing their clothes in the river, they called across to the Christian women on the other side. "What were those strange lights in your huts last night?" they asked.

"What lights?" the Christian women replied. "We had no lights burning. We were all asleep."[41]

26
Lifeguard Angels

More than sixty years ago, when I was a boy, one landmark in our town was the millrace on the Cedar River. In the midst of the millrace was a giant pipe, positioned to keep the river debris from rushing downstream. A giant screen had been attached to the pipe's outlet. Here, the debris could be halted, and every few months the screen would be removed and cleaned.

There were warning signs along the millrace bank: *Danger, Strong Current, Undertow, Swimming Strictly Forbidden.* But you know how boys are.

It was full-river season, with extra danger because the water was high. But into the water I went. Before I knew what had happened, I was swept into the pipe, sucked under the water by the powerful rush of the millrace! I was about to drown.

Then suddenly I felt a lift, as though a hand were taking me up to the air.

I filled my lungs and fought against the undertow. But still I was little competition for the downward pull. Down to the bottom again. Then came that hand again. Something, *someone* lifted me up for air again. Three or four times it happened. I kept struggling, turning around, heading back toward the entrance. Yet with each turn now I seemed to hear a voice saying, "Forget the screen! Head for the outward exit!" Then once more I felt the hand, this time turning me hard, hurling me toward the screen end. With one mighty shove, up, up, and out of the tunnel, up to unlimited air.

I do not remember all that happened then, but this one thing I will never forget. As they pulled me into their boat, the lifeguard said, "Were you ever lucky, kid. Yesterday we took the screen off to clean the thing."

Then the captain asked a question: *"Weren't two of you in there? Somehow we got the idea there were two."* [42]

27

The Awesome Being

Reverend L. Larson told of a woman in his congregation, Myrna Martinson, who was awakened from sleep by a beautiful spirit being who told her to pray. She did as she was bade and continued in earnest prayer for an hour or more. At last a feeling of tranquillity came over her, and she fell back asleep.

A few hours later, Mrs. Martinson was awakened from her sleep once again—the second time by a startling telephone call that informed her that at the very time she had been praying, her nine-year-old daughter, Tammy, who was away in the city visiting her grandparents, was trapped in their burning home.

The fireman who rescued the girl said that he found the child's bedroom completely enveloped in flames—except for the corner in which Tammy crouched. Standing protectively over the girl, the fireman swore, was "an awesome being, all white and silvery," who withdrew at his approach and seemed to turn over the rescue of the girl to his professional firefighter's skills.

Later, after she had spent some time breathing from an oxygen mask, Tammy corroborated the fireman's perceptions of the "awesome" silvery and white being.

"He was my guardian angel," she said simply. "And he protected me from the fire until the big fireman came."[43]

28

Margaret and the Dobermans

It was about a mile from Margaret's house to the dentist's office, and since it was a nice day she decided to walk to her appointment.

Just as Margaret got to the rise of a knoll at the end of the residential part of the street, two snarly Doberman pinschers charged out of their front yard. They sandwiched Margaret between them and edged forward in an attack posture.

Traffic was thick, but car after car passed without noticing Margaret's predicament.

Suddenly a young man leaped from a shiny black pick-up truck that appeared showroom-new. He strode through the traffic and took immediate command of the situation. With a word and a gesture he broke up the melee and sent the dogs yelping back to their yard. He then turned and walked straight through the traffic back to his truck.

Margaret was momentarily stunned by the total authority shown by the mysterious stranger, and, noticing that he had paused to make a left turn into the parking lot, she hurried to catch up with him.

She saw him turn, but when she got to the spot where both she and the driver should have arrived simultaneously, there was nothing—absolutely no sign of any person or truck. The young man and the shiny black truck had vanished without a trace.[44]

29

Angels to the Rescue?

My father was going up a small grade on his tractor when all at once the tractor reared up and over. My father could not get off. He hung on and ended up under the tractor. What could he do?

It is lucky my father is a strong man and his legs are his strongest part. When it happened, I ran out to the field. There he was holding the tractor up with his legs. It was not a big tractor, but big enough. I didn't know what to do. Then all at once here came two men running across the field.

If you saw where we live, you would wonder where these two came from. The only road by our house is gravel and hardly anybody drives on it. We don't have close neighbors and we're a long way from town. But here they came. When they got to us it didn't take them hardly any time at all to lift up the tractor for my father to crawl out. Of course my father thanked them and invited them to dinner at our house. But they said they couldn't come because they had to be going. Dad asked their names but they just waved and went off down the road. We didn't see a car, a truck, or anything to ride in.[45]

30

Why Are There Angels?

Why are there angels? Why does God need them—or us? In a certain sense, if God is God, then there *must* be angels. God is the ultimate team player, starting with his very nature: he's three Persons existing and working as One God. It's almost as though angels—and human beings—are the necessary creative expressions of the nature of God. Because God is the way he is, he wouldn't have it any other way. He created human persons and angels to partner with him in his created order. God doesn't "need" angels, but he uses them![46]

∞

So often, people who have seen angels speak of the light that they seem to radiate. An angel's light has been provided by God, who *is* light. ("God is Light, pure light; there's not a trace of darkness in him.")[47]

So the angels are acting as Light-refractors, heavenly prisms.

∞

Jesus Christ has gone into heaven and is at God's right hand— with angels, authorities, and powers in submission to him.[48]

31

An Angel Surprised a Centurion

At Caesarea there was a man named Cornelius, a centurion. He and all his family were devout and God-fearing; he gave generously to those in need and prayed to God regularly. One day at about three in the afternoon he had a vision. He distinctly saw an angel of God, who came to him and said, "Cornelius!"

Cornelius stared at him in fear. "What is it, Lord?" he asked.

The angel answered, "Your prayers and gifts to the poor have come up as a memorial offering before God. Now send men to Joppa to bring back a man named Simon who is called Peter. He is staying with Simon the tanner, whose house is by the sea."

When the angel who spoke to him had gone, Cornelius called two of his servants and a devout soldier who was one of his attendants. He told them everything that had happened and sent them to Joppa.

The men sent by Cornelius found out where Simon's house was and stopped at the gate. They called out, asking if Simon who was known as Peter was staying there.

Peter went down and said to the men, "I'm the one you're looking for. Why have you come?"

The men replied, "We have come from Cornelius the centurion. He is a righteous and God-fearing man, who is respected by all the Jewish people. A holy angel told him to have you come to his house so that he could hear what you have to say." Then Peter invited the men into the house to be his guests.[49]

32

Angels Never Get in God's Way

Have you ever wondered why it happens that angels appear most frequently in the guise of ordinary human beings rather than the heavenly, barely embodied creatures we sometimes are privileged to see? I think it's because they don't want us to focus on them any longer than necessary, but on the message they bring and the One from whom the message comes. Whenever we receive some kind of message that does not move us in some way closer to God—whether that means we pray or thank God aloud or whether we communicate our love and thanks in some less articulate fashion—then we should look to ourselves and our own creative abilities for the source of the message.

If the messenger is so opaquely between us and the message or the Sender that we see only the messenger, then the messenger is not an angel. I can't emphasize that enough. Angels never stand in the way. Angels are prisms who let the light, the message through. They are clear glass, only noticeable until the sun comes up and shines in the window. They do not want to be the focus of our attention for any longer than it takes to deliver their message or do whatever they have been sent to do.[50]

33

Angels Are No Substitute for God

A ngels are not affected personally by the pain and evil that still exist on earth.... However, one thing does affect them—when we mistakenly think of them as substitutes for the Light, as mini-gods, as beings to be worshiped or placated. For an angel, this is as close to pain as is possible.[51]

∞

It is very right that these blessed and immortal spirits, who inhabit celestial dwellings and rejoice in the communications of their Creator's fullness, firm in his eternity, assured in his truth, holy by his grace, since they compassionately and tenderly regard us miserable mortals, and wish us to become immortal and happy, do not desire us to sacrifice to themselves, but to him whose sacrifice they know themselves to be in common with us. For we and they together are the one city of God, to which it is said in the psalm, "Glorious things are spoken of thee, O city of God"; the human part sojourning here below, the angelic aiding from above. It is written, "He that sacrificeth unto any god, save to the Lord only, he shall be utterly destroyed." This Scripture has been confirmed by such miracles, that it is sufficiently evident to whom these immortal and blessed spirits, who desire us to be like themselves, wish us to sacrifice.[52]

34

O Come, Let Us Adore Him

We bless you, our Stronghold, our King and Redeemer, Creator of holy beings. May your name forever be praised, our King, Creator of ministering angels, all of whom stand at the heights of the universe and reverently declaim, together and with one voice the words of the living God, the everlasting King. All of them are beloved, all of them are pure, all of them are strong; they all perform with awe and reverence the will of their Creator; they all open their mouth with holiness and purity, with song and melody, while they bless and praise, glorify and revere, sanctify and acclaim the name of the great, mighty, and awesome God and King.[53]

∞

Sing, choirs of angels,
Sing in exultation,
O sing, all ye bright hosts of heav'n above!
Glory to God,
All glory in the highest!
O come, let us adore him,
Christ the Lord![54]

∞

Praise the LORD, you his angels,
you mighty ones who do his bidding,
who obey his word.[55]

35

The Angels' Foremost Activity

Without ceasing, the angels praise and glorify God. Because they were created to praise him, their endless worship is supernaturally natural. The angels are, in Dante's words, an "army which beholds and sings the glory of the One who stirs its love."[56]

∞

The angels have the affection and desire to be wise. All their thoughts and affections flow in accordance with divine wisdom. Nothing withdraws them from the divine influx, and nothing external intrudes from other thoughts, as with man. The thoughts of the angels are not, like human thoughts, bounded and contracted by ideas derived from space and time. Nor are the thoughts of angels drawn down to earthly and material things; nor interrupted by any cares about the necessaries of life. Thus they are not withdrawn by these things from the delights of wisdom, as the thoughts of men are in the world. For all things come to them without recompense from the Lord; they are clothed without recompense, they are nourished without recompense, they have habitations without recompense. And moreover they are gifted with delights and pleasures according to their reception of wisdom from the Lord.[57]

36

The Wedding of the Lamb

I heard what sounded like the roar of a great multitude in heaven shouting: "Hallelujah! Salvation and glory and power belong to our God, for true and just are his judgments. He has condemned the great prostitute who corrupted the earth by her adulteries. He has avenged on her the blood of his servants."

And again they shouted: "Hallelujah! The smoke from her goes up for ever and ever."

The twenty-four elders and the four living creatures fell down and worshiped God, who was seated on the throne. And they cried: "Amen, Hallelujah!"

Then a voice came from the throne, saying: "Praise our God, all you his servants, you who fear him, both small and great!"

Then I heard what sounded like a great multitude, like the roar of rushing waters and like loud peals of thunder, shouting: "Hallelujah! For our Lord God Almighty reigns. Let us rejoice and be glad and give him glory! For the wedding of the Lamb has come, and his bride has made herself ready."

Then the angel said to me, "Write: 'Blessed are those who are invited to the wedding supper of the Lamb!'"[58]

37

Angels Are a Unique Creation

Angels are not a society of glorified human beings. They do not represent the ultimate growth potential of the human spirit. Not a single human being has ever become or will ever become an angel, no matter how pure or holy or evolved he or she might grow to be. Do oak trees evolve into giraffes? Can a mountain become a beluga whale if given enough time? Can oxygen evolve into a cat? No, each is a unique type of creation, and while each may change or grow, it does so according to the natural laws that govern its species. The ancient writings are clear that angels are a separate species, one that predates the human race.[59]

∞

Angels are not humans who have died, whether babies or adults. According to Colossians 1:16, angels are among the invisible beings created by God. Each angel has been directly created by God from nothing. Angels do not give birth to baby angels. The only way an angel has ever come into existence is to have been created by God. People are *born*. Angels are *created*.

Angels do not die. Once God has created an angel, the angel continues to exist. On earth, if people had not had children, within a generation everyone would have died and there would be no one on earth. It is not like that with angels. God did not make them able to reproduce, because there is no reason for them to do so. God has created every angel necessary, and they all continue to be, to this day.[60]

38

Michael Faces Lucifer

Lucifer: Riddle me this. If the Tyrant [God] would allow men to be "sons of God," then why not gods?

Michael: That is the line which can never be crossed. Angels are angels. They can stay in heaven or fall like lightning, but they can never be gods. At the crossing of that line all death enters in. The sons of God may not become or aspire to be gods. That is death.

Lucifer: I disagree! That is divinity and I have many gods. Even in the church. Proud, fierce, unruled, self-willed, greedy, slothful, glorious gods. They teach one another to become gods. They speak as gods of their own desires, and in envious wrath wreak havoc in his house. Mine, mine, mine! And they do not even know it. What sublime delight. They think because they do not worship me that they are not of me. I care nothing for their worship. I only want them to be gods. For I am god and the god of all gods; all gods are of me.

Michael: You? You are defined only as "not what you were." You are the fallen one. Unredeemable. Unrepentant. Rebel. The fire awaits you. Nothing else. But for them there is still hope. There is a balm in Gilead. Good-bye, Lucifer.

Lucifer: Shall we not meet again? I do so love our little chats.

Michael: Meet again? To be sure, but not for a chat. At God's command, our brother Gabriel shall lift the trump and summon you to your reward.[61]

39

The Sound of Wings

Courage is the price that life exacts for granting peace.
The soul that knows it not, knows no release
From little things;
Knows not the livid loneliness of fear,
Nor mountain heights where bitter joy can hear
The sound of wings.[62]

∞

O world invisible, we view thee,
O world intangible, we touch thee,
O world unknowable, we know thee,
Inapprehensible, we clutch thee!...

The angels keep their ancient places;
Turn but a stone and start a wing!
'Tis ye, 'tis your estrangèd faces,
that miss the many-splendoured thing.[63]

40

All on Fire

Teresa of Avila, a reformer within the church of Spain in the 16th century, was a great woman of prayer. Catholics and Protestants alike appreciate her profound, biblically based writing on spirituality.

As Teresa grew in intimacy with God, she repeatedly experienced an extraordinary palpable sign of her closeness to him. It was as though God were literally taking possession of her heart and setting it aflame with love. And once he sent an angel on assignment to communicate his love to her.

Following is her own description of the divine invasion of her soul: "I saw an angel close by me, on my left side, in bodily form. He was not large, but small of stature and most beautiful—his face burning, as if he were one of the highest angels, who seem to be all of fire.... I saw in his hand a long spear of gold, and at the iron's point there seemed to be a little flame. He appeared to me to be thrusting it at times into my heart, and to pierce my very entrails; when he drew it out, he seemed to draw them out also, and to leave me all on fire with the great love of God."

The popular mind identifies this vision with Teresa. Artists and sculptors have often depicted it, the most famous representation being the seventeenth-century statue by Giovanni Bernini.

Words cannot describe what really happened to Teresa. She says that God touched her heart in a delightful yet painful way, leaving her soul afire with love for him. An astonishing fact witnessed to the truth of her words: according to a physician's testimony, after her death, Teresa's heart was found to bear a long, deep scar.[64]

41
No Angel Families

Humans, according to the Bible, are organically related to one another in that we are all descendants of "one person," as Acts 17:26 and Romans 5:12-21 indicate. Furthermore, we are intimately related to a specific family because we are born from human parents who themselves come from parents, and so on.

As far as we can tell, such organic relationships do not exist among angels. In response to a question of the Sadducees about marriage in the resurrection, Jesus says: "When the dead rise, they will neither marry nor be given in marriage; they will be like the angels in heaven" (Mark 12:25, or see parallel passages Matthew 22:30; Luke 9:35-36). What seems to be underlying this teaching is the understanding that angels do not participate in marriage the way we humans do. There are no "little" angels who are born from other angels, no "good" angels who serve God as their parents did.

The fact is, there seems to be no "male" and "female" in the angelic world. All of the references to angels in the Bible seem to be male: "he" is the personal pronoun used, and the angels generally take on the bodily appearance of men when they are used to tell the gospel story of the coming of the kingdom. (Interestingly, today when we want a group to sing as "a choir of angels," we choose females for the parts. Either our idea of angels has changed, or males no longer are able to convey that they are a choir of angels!) The important thing to consider is that whatever commitment angels have to one another, their clear and total commitment is to the service of God and the revelation of the coming kingdom.[65]

42

"Send Some of Your Angels"

In 1952, Frank was a naval officer stationed in Europe. We were driving with our family through thick fog in the Swiss Alps when a gap in the road, about six feet wide and four feet deep, confronted us. Night was coming on, so Frank walked the others down to the next village. Since all our belongings were in the car, I stayed behind. I waited. Nervously I tried to pray. The words of Psalms 91:11-12 came to mind: "For he shall give his angels charge over thee... They shall bear thee up in their hands...." And then I blurted out, "Lord, *send some of your angels*. Please."

A truck suddenly appeared. Out of it piled six big, rough-looking bearded men. Without speaking, they picked up their truck and carried it across the washout. Then with strong, powerful hands they picked up *my* car—with me in it—carried it across the trench, and set it safely on the other side. They never said a word, and disappeared into the night.

I drove into the village of Brig, where I found my family. Nobody in the village could imagine who those men were. All I knew was that they had come, and they had borne me up "in their hands."[66]

∞

Do not forget to entertain strangers, for by so doing some people have entertained angels without knowing it.[67]

43
Angel Conversation

I climbed into bed with some anxiety, praying one more time for guidance and help before going to sleep. I was more or less resolved to confront a Christian friend in the morning about a persistent sinful habit. However, I was much younger than she. If God really wanted me to do it, I would initiate such a conversation, although to me it was a very difficult assignment.

In the middle of the night, a small noise woke me. I listened in the pitch blackness. Then, with intense interest replacing any fear, I saw two faces in lighted profile, talking to each other. I heard just a snatch of their conversation:

"Is she really going to do it?"
"Yes!"

Somehow I knew that these were angels, "on assignment." Even without further evidence of their presence in the room, I felt enormously reassured to go ahead the next day and do what I felt God wanted. I fell asleep again, filled with peace and resolve.

It almost goes without saying that the "confrontation" was successful. My older friend later told me that it marked a turning point in her life.[68]

44

Angels Bring God's Truth to His People

Angels are supernatural apparitions, raised by the special and extraordinary operation of God, thereby to make his presence and commandments known to mankind, and chiefly to his own people.[69]

∞

Then the angel showed me the Water-of-Life River, crystal bright. It flowed from the Throne of God and the Lamb, right down the middle of the street. The Tree of Life was planted on each side of the River, producing twelve kinds of fruit, a ripe fruit each month. The leaves of the Tree are for healing the nations. Never again will anything be cursed. The Throne of God and of the Lamb is at its center. His servants will offer God service—worshiping, they'll look on his face, their foreheads mirroring God. Never again will there be any night. No one will need lamplight or sunlight. The shining of God, the Master, is all the light anyone needs. And they will rule with him age after age after age.

The angel said to me, "These are dependable and accurate words, every one. The God and Master of the spirits of the prophets sent his angel to show his servants what must take place, and soon."[70]

∞

To which of the angels did God ever say, "Sit at my right hand until I make your enemies a footstool for your feet"? Are not all angels ministering spirits sent to serve those who will inherit salvation?[71]

45

God's Angel "Sees" Hagar

The angel of the Lord found Hagar near a spring in the desert; it was the spring that is beside the road to Shur. And he said, "Hagar, servant of Sarai, where have you come from, and where are you going?"

"I'm running away from my mistress Sarai," she answered.

Then the angel of the Lord told her, "Go back to your mistress and submit to her." The angel added, "I will so increase your descendants that they will be too numerous to count."

The angel of the Lord also said to her:

> "You are now with child
> and you will have a son.
> You shall name him Ishmael,
> for the Lord has heard of your misery.
> He will be a wild donkey of a man;
> his hand will be against everyone
> and everyone's hand against him,
> and he will live in hostility
> toward all his brothers."

She gave this name to the Lord who spoke to her: "You are the God who sees me," for she said, "I have now seen the One who sees me."[72]

46

Gabriel Makes a Promise to Zechariah

There was a priest named Zechariah, who belonged to the priestly division of Abijah; his wife Elizabeth was also a descendant of Aaron. Both of them were upright in the sight of God, observing all the Lord's commandments and regulations blamelessly. But they had no children, because Elizabeth was barren; and they were both well along in years.

Once when Zechariah was serving as priest before God, he was chosen by lot to go into the temple of the Lord and burn incense.

Then an angel of the Lord appeared to him, standing at the right side of the altar of incense. When Zechariah saw him, he was startled and was gripped with fear. But the angel said to him: "Do not be afraid, Zechariah; your prayer has been heard. Your wife Elizabeth will bear you a son, and you are to give him the name John. He will be a joy and delight to you, and many will rejoice because of his birth, for he will be great in the sight of the Lord. And he will go on before the Lord, in the spirit and power of Elijah, to turn the hearts of the fathers to their children and the disobedient to the wisdom of the righteous—to make ready a people prepared for the Lord."

Zechariah asked the angel, "How can I be sure of this? I am an old man and my wife is well along in years."

The angel answered, "I am Gabriel. I stand in the presence of God, and I have been sent to speak to you and to tell you this good news."[73]

47

An Angel Ministers to Elijah

Ahab told Jezebel everything Elijah had done and how he had killed all the prophets with the sword. So Jezebel sent a messenger to Elijah to say, "May the gods deal with me, be it ever so severely, if by this time tomorrow I do not make your life like that of one of them."

Elijah was afraid and ran for his life. When he came to Beersheba in Judah, he left his servant there, while he himself went a day's journey into the desert. He came to a broom tree, sat down under it and prayed that he might die. "I have had enough, Lord," he said. "Take my life; I am no better than my ancestors." Then he lay down under the tree and fell asleep.

All at once an angel touched him and said, "Get up and eat." He looked around, and there by his head was a cake of bread baked over hot coals, and a jar of water. He ate and drank and then lay down again.

The angel of the Lord came back a second time and touched him and said, "Get up and eat, for the journey is too much for you." So he got up and ate and drank. Strengthened by that food, he traveled forty days and forty nights until he reached Horeb, the mountain of God.[74]

48
Jacob's Ladder

Jacob left Beersheba and journeyed toward Haran. That night, when he stopped to camp at sundown, he found a rock for a head-rest and lay down to sleep, and dreamed that a ladder reached from earth to heaven, and he saw angels of God going up and down upon it.

At the top of the stairs stood the Lord. "I am Jehovah," he said, "the God of Abraham, and of your father Isaac. The ground you are lying on is yours! I will give it to you and to your descendants. For you will have descendants as many as dust! They will cover the land from east to west and from north to south; and all the nations of the earth will be blessed through you and your descendants. What's more, I am with you, and will protect you wherever you go, and will bring you back safely to this land; I will be with you constantly until I have finished giving you all I am promising."

Then Jacob woke up. "God lives here!" he exclaimed in terror. "I've stumbled into his home! This is the awesome entrance to heaven!" The next morning he got up very early and set his stone headrest upright as a memorial pillar, and poured olive oil over it.[75]

49

Angels Are Links to God

Angels are not like minor gods, although they are supernatural beings. God's angels are as distinct from God himself as they are from the human race. But their mission is forever linked with both heaven and earth—they serve as links between God and human beings.

The Jewish people had ignored repeated warnings to turn away from their sin or face the consequences. Obstinate in their disregard for God, these stiff-necked people were finally conquered by one of the ancient world's most powerful nations: dreadful Babylon. As a result, Daniel and many others like him were forced into captivity, exiled from their beloved Jerusalem.

But Daniel never sulked or complained about his predicament, insisting that he was being punished unfairly. Instead, he knelt before God and beseeched him to have mercy on his people. Though Daniel had not himself sinned, he stood with those who had, humbling himself and repenting of their sin. Evidently, God could not resist the prayers of such a man. The angel Gabriel actually told Daniel that a word went out from heaven because of his prayer. And whenever God speaks a word, things really do begin to happen. Incredible as it seems, we learn from this story that our prayers can actually set heaven in motion. Sometimes they even have the power to dispatch angels with a message of wisdom.[76]

50
Saved from the Lions

The administrators went to the king and said: "The king should issue an edict and enforce the decree that anyone who prays to any god or man during the next thirty days, except to you, O king, shall be thrown into the lions' den. Now, issue the decree and put it in writing so that it cannot be altered." So King Darius put the decree in writing.

When Daniel learned that the decree had been published, he went home to his upstairs room where the windows opened toward Jerusalem. Three times a day he got down on his knees and prayed, giving thanks to his God, just as he had done before. Then these men went as a group and found Daniel praying and asking God for help. So they went to the king and spoke to him about his royal decree: "Did you not publish a decree that during the next thirty days anyone who prays to any god or man except to you would be thrown into the lions' den?"

The king answered, "The decree stands."

So they brought Daniel and threw him into the lions' den.

At dawn, the king hurried to the den and called, "Daniel, servant of the living God, has your God, whom you serve continually, been able to rescue you from the lions?"

Daniel answered, "My God sent his angel, and he shut the mouths of the lions. They have not hurt me, because I was found innocent in his sight."

When Daniel was lifted from the den, no wound was found on him, because he had trusted in his God.[77]

51

The Most Amazing Angelic
Message of All Time

In the sixth month, God sent the angel Gabriel to Nazareth, a town in Galilee, to a virgin pledged to be married to a man named Joseph, a descendant of David. The virgin's name was Mary. The angel went to her and said, "Greetings, you who are highly favored! The Lord is with you."

Mary was greatly troubled at his words and wondered what kind of greeting this might be. But the angel said to her, "Do not be afraid, Mary, you have found favor with God. You will be with child and give birth to a son, and you are to give him the name Jesus. He will be great and will be called the Son of the Most High. The Lord God will give him the throne of his father David, and he will reign over the house of Jacob forever; his kingdom will never end."

"How will this be," Mary asked the angel, "since I am a virgin?"

The angel answered, "The Holy Spirit will come upon you, and the power of the Most High will overshadow you. So the holy one to be born will be called the Son of God. Even Elizabeth your relative is going to have a child in her old age, and she who was said to be barren is in her sixth month. For nothing is impossible with God."

"I am the Lord's servant," Mary answered. "May it be to me as you have said." Then the angel left her.[78]

52

The Angels Sing

It came upon the midnight clear,
That glorious song of old,
From angels bending near the earth
To touch their harps of gold;
"Peace on the earth, good-will to men,
From heav'n's all-gracious King."
The world in solemn stillness lay
To hear the angels sing.

Still thro' the cloven skies they come,
With peaceful wings unfurled,
And still their heav'nly music floats
O'er all the weary world:
Above its sad and lowly plains
They bend on hov'ring wing:
And ever o'er its Babel sounds
The blessed angels sing.

And ye, beneath life's crushing load,
Whose forms are bending low,
Who toil along the climbing way
With painful steps and slow,
Look now! for glad and golden hours
Come swiftly on the wing;
O rest beside the weary road,
And hear the angels sing.

For lo, the days are hast'ning on,
By prophet bards foretold,
When with the ever-circling years
Comes round the age of gold;
When peace shall over all the earth
Its ancient splendors fling,
And the whole world give back the song
Which now the angels sing.[79]

53

Angels Announce Jesus' Birth

In Scripture the visitation of an angel is always alarming; it has to begin by saying "Fear not."[80]

∞

There were shepherds camping in the neighborhood. They had set night watches over their sheep. Suddenly, God's angel stood among them and God's glory blazed around them. They were terrified. The angel said, "Don't be afraid. I'm here to announce a great and joyful event that is meant for everybody worldwide: A Savior has just been born in David's town, a Savior who is Messiah and Master. This is what you're to look for: a baby wrapped in a blanket and lying in a manger."

At once the angel was joined by a huge angelic choir singing God's praises:

"Glory to God in the heavenly heights,
Peace to all men and women on earth who please him."

As the angel choir withdrew into heaven, the shepherds talked it over. "Let's get over to Bethlehem as fast as we can and see for ourselves what God has revealed to us."[81]

∞

Hark! the herald angels sing,
"Glory to the newborn King;
Peace on earth, and mercy mild;
God and sinners reconciled."
Joyful, all ye nations rise,
Join the triumph of the skies;
With th'angelic hosts proclaim,
"Christ is born in Bethlehem."[82]

54

Angels Seek Humble Hearts

Imagine the shepherds' astonishment to look up and see the night sky peppered with angels. Luke's Gospel tells us that the first angel was suddenly joined by "a great company of the heavenly host." The angels didn't announce the good news of Jesus' birth to any of the prominent people of Israel. They didn't appear to the mayor or the chief of police or even to King Herod in nearby Jerusalem, but to shepherds, plain men who stood guard over their noisy charges in the fields.

So often in Scripture, we see that God is not impressed with the things that impress us. He seems to go to great lengths to drive this point home: his Son was born to an ordinary Jewish couple; Mary and Joseph were poor people; Jesus lived most of his life in obscurity.

The angels had a message to deliver and they must have known that it would take root best in the soil of humility. So they told the shepherds about the Good Shepherd who would one day save them from their sins. And the shepherds believed.

The story of the shepherds convinces me that God is irresistibly attracted to humble hearts. It's as though the law of gravity has a spiritual equivalent. An object thrown from a high building will speed on until it hits the ground. So it is with God's grace as it courses from heaven to earth, coming to rest finally in the hearts of lowly men and women.[83]

55
The Newborn King

While shepherds watched their flocks by night,
All seated on the ground,
The angel of the Lord came down,
And glory shone around.

"Fear not!" said he; for mighty dread
Had seized their troubled mind,
"Glad tidings of great joy I bring,
To you and all mankind.

"To you, in David's town, this day
Is born, of David's line,
The Savior, who is Christ the Lord;
And this shall be the sign:

"All glory be to God on high,
And to the earth be peace:
Good-will henceforth from heav'n to men,
Begin and never cease!"[84]

∞

Angels, from the realms of glory,
Wing your flight o'er all the earth;
Ye, who sang creation's story,
Now proclaim Messiah's birth;
Come and worship, come and worship,
Worship Christ, the newborn King.[85]

56

Our Angels Perceive What We Do Not

The writer of the Letter to the Hebrews makes it abundantly clear that angels worship Jesus as the firstborn of the new creation. Jesus is not simply a bit greater than the angels, but infinitely superior to them. Knowing this, the angels adore him.

It seems fitting that the earth would have thrilled the moment its Maker became incarnate. True, there were angels and a star of some brilliance that guided the wise men, and yet we know of nothing more spectacular: no earthquakes or floods or meteor showers to herald the event. There was no cheering crowd, no glitzy birthday bash, no front-page story in the *Jerusalem Post*.

Yet the angels were there. They knew exactly what was going on. They witnessed what the world would not or could not. And they shared the good news of his coming with the shepherds in the field.

Like the sun behind the clouds, Jesus is a living reality whether we perceive him or not. Though sometimes hidden from us, he is not hidden from our angels. When we want so badly to sense that he is with us, let us take comfort in knowing that our angels perceive what we do not. Knowing this, we can pray that God will open our eyes and hearts to his presence.[86]

57
Glorious Designs

God is forever imaginative, colorful, and glorious in what he designs. Some of the descriptions of angels, including the one of Lucifer, indicate that they are exotic to the human eye and mind. Apparently angels have a beauty and variety that surpass anything known to men.[87]

∞

"The Lord God says: 'You were the perfection of wisdom and beauty. You were in Eden, the garden of God; your clothing was bejeweled with every precious stone—ruby, topaz, diamond, chrysolite, onyx, jasper, sapphire, carbuncle, and emerald—all in beautiful settings of finest gold. They were given to you on the day you were created. I appointed you to be the anointed Guardian Angel. You had access to the holy mountain of God. You walked among the stones of fire.

"'You were perfect in all you did from the day you were created until that time when wrong was found in you. Your great wealth filled you with internal turmoil, and you sinned. Therefore, I cast you out of the mountain of God like a common sinner. I destroyed you, O Guardian Angel, from the midst of the stones of fire. Your heart was filled with pride because of all your beauty; you corrupted your wisdom for the sake of your splendor. You defiled your holiness with lust for gain; therefore, I brought forth fire from your own actions and let it burn you to ashes upon the earth in the sight of all those watching you. All who know you are appalled at your fate; you are an example of horror; you are destroyed forever.'"[88]

58

A Wonder to Behold

The sky spreading out above them looked as though it were made of crystal; it was inexpressibly beautiful.

The wings of each stretched straight out to touch the others' wings, and each had two wings covering his body. And as they flew, their wings roared like waves against the shore, or like the voice of God, or like the shouting of a mighty army. When they stopped, they let down their wings.[89]

> O, speak again, bright angel, for thou art
> As glorious to this night, being o'er my head,
> As is a winged messenger of heaven
> Unto the white-upturned wond'ring eyes
> Of mortals that fall back to gaze on him,
> When he bestrides the lazy puffing clouds,
> And sails upon the bosoms of the air.[90]

After this I saw another angel coming down from heaven. He had great authority, and the earth was illuminated by his splendor.[91]

59
Ezekiel's Vision of the Living Beings

I saw a great storm coming toward me from the north, driving before it a huge cloud glowing with fire, with a mass of fire inside that flashed continually; and in the fire there was something that shone like polished brass.

Then from the center of the cloud, four strange forms appeared that looked like men, except that each had four faces and two pairs of wings! Their legs were like those of men, but their feet were cloven like calves' feet, and shone like burnished brass. And beneath each of their wings I could see human hands.

The four living beings were joined wing to wing, and they flew straight forward without turning. Each had the face of a man [in front], with a lion's face on the right side [of his head], and the face of an ox on the left side, and the face of an eagle at the back! Each had two pairs of wings spreading out from the middle of his back. One pair stretched out to attach to the wings of the living beings on each side, and the other pair covered his body. Wherever their spirit went they went, going straight forward without turning.

Going up and down among them were other forms that glowed like bright coals of fire or brilliant torches, and it was from these the lightning flashed. The living beings darted to and fro, swift as lightning.[92]

60
Angels Dazzle

Angels are beings of dazzling, sometimes blinding, light, suggesting that their home is in heaven in the bright, resplendent presence of God. Something of God has rubbed onto them.[93]

∞

Just as the sun is the central light for our solar system, God is the supreme light of the spiritual world. Angels are secondary or reflecting lights, pulsating his presence. They are so "imprinted" with God's light as perfect servants of the divine will that they, in turn, become lights themselves.

Angels as bearers of God's message and presence are usually so impressive because of the extraordinary light or brilliance of their being.[94]

∞

An angel of the Lord came down from heaven and, going to the tomb, rolled back the stone and sat on it. His appearance was like lightning, and his clothes were white as snow.[95]

61
Blinding Light

I saw that noble host of souls, who now
in silence kept their eyes raised to the heavens,
as if expectant, faces pale and meek,

and then I saw descending from on high
two angels with two flaming swords, and these
were broken short and blunted at the end.

Their garments, green as tender new-born leaves
unfurling, billowed out behind each one,
fanned by the greenness of their streaming wings.

One took his stand above us on our side,
and one alighted on the other bank;
thus, all the souls were held between the two.

My eyes could see with ease their golden hair,
but could not bear the radiance of their faces;
light that makes visible can also blind.[96]

62

"I Felt Such Love Reaching Out Toward Me..."

I felt a presence, and I looked up, and it seemed to me as though the entire end of the room had opened up, and a light was growing in its place. The back wall, the floor, the ceiling—all faded away, to be replaced by the most incredibly beautiful light I have ever seen. The light was so intense I could hardly stand it, at first.

And standing there in the midst of the light appeared a very quivering, vibrating, pulsating being of light with outstretched wings that curved down a bit at the tips, as though they were reaching out to embrace me, and a face that was very loving. And although the figure itself shone with an intensely bright, vibrant, transparent white light, the wings and the head and the angel's face were colored like the northern lights, the aurora borealis. I saw such beautiful colors—pink, yellow, green, white, and gold, sparkling and vibrating. The light was very solid—I couldn't see anything beyond it.

I felt such love reaching out toward me and all around me as I had never experienced before. I had the sensation of knowing that I was never alone, that this being was always with me in some way to comfort me. The face was full of compassion, loving, soft, and gentle. There was a tremendous love energy in the room, and I was filled with that mystical presence.[97]

63

A Face Like a Trembling Star

L ook over there, and see. The angel comes!
And, see—the sixth handmaiden has returned
already from her service to the day.

Show reverence in your face and attitude,
so that he will be glad to help us up;
think that this day will never dawn again!"

Still closer to us, clothed in white, he came,
the radiantly fair creature, and his face
was shining like a trembling star at dawn.

He spread his arms out wide, and then his wings.
He said: "Come, now, the steps are very close;
henceforth, the climbing will be easier."

To such an invitation few respond:
O race of men, born to fly heavenward,
how can a breath of wind make you fall back?

He led us straight to where the rock was cleft,
Once there, he brushed his wings against my brow,
then he assured me of a safe ascent.[98]

64
Lighted by an Angel Crew?

The Home for the Dying in Calcutta is operated by the Sisters of Charity, led by the now-famous Mother Teresa. In 1969, Malcolm Muggeridge, before writing his biography of Mother Teresa, *Something Beautiful for God,* travelled to Calcutta with a crew from the BBC to film a documentary about the work of this remarkable nun.

In order to film the actual work of the sisters, the crew needed to bring their equipment into the dimly lit interior of the Home for the Dying. The only existing light came from small windows high up in the walls, and the cameraman had only one inadequate light with him. It was decided that he would give it a try in spite of the impossible light conditions, but to redeem the rest of the film, he also took some pictures in the sunny outside courtyard.

When the film was developed, the portion which had been shot indoors was bathed in a particularly beautiful soft light, whereas the part taken in the courtyard was somewhat dim and confused.

"I am convinced that the technically unaccountable light is, in fact, supernatural," Muggeridge wrote. "Mother Teresa's Home for the Dying is overflowing with a luminous love.... The light conveys perfectly what the place is really like; an outward and visible luminosity manifesting God's inward and invisible omnipresent love.... I find it not at all surprising that the luminosity should register on a photographic film."[99]

65

Angels Come in All Forms

Limited as we are to our steadily aging bodies, we find it fascinating that angels can take any form that suits the message. A "classic" angel, with wings and all lighted up, perhaps with pale skin and eyes of blue flame, seems to be less often glimpsed than do angels in the guise of ordinary folks of all sorts—male or female, young or old, tall or short, any race, any dialect, any description.

Of course, angels are often not seen, but rather felt or heard or sensed. People recount a shifting color in the atmosphere, a dream, a clarifying thought, a surge of superhuman strength. Sometimes only visible is the tip of a sword or a muscular arm flung out protectively.

Masters of disguise because their Master is the Creator of everything visible and invisible, angels do their jobs well. And if you see one, you yourself are changed.

∞

As Joshua was sizing up the city of Jericho, a man appeared nearby with a drawn sword. Joshua strode over to him and demanded, "Are you friend or foe?"

"Neither. I am the Commander-in-Chief of the Lord's army," he replied.

Joshua fell to the ground before him and worshiped and said, "Give me your commands."

"Take off your shoes," the Commander told him, "for this is holy ground." And Joshua did.[100]

66
The Angel Dog

When I was six years old, there was a big forest behind our house. One day a black squirrel came in our yard. I had never seen a black squirrel, so when he ran into the woods I followed, and pretty soon I was lost. It seemed like every way I went the woods just got thicker. I put my face in my hands and cried and prayed.

All of a sudden I felt something licking my face. I was almost scared to open my eyes, but I did. It was a big brown-and-white dog. He was huge, the biggest dog I'd ever seen.

He stopped licking my face and started pulling on my skirt. After a long time he brought me to my very own back porch. I ran into the kitchen, and my parents were so glad to see me they didn't even scold me. We all ran outside to see my new friend, but he was gone. We live in a very little town so my parents asked everybody if they had seen a big brown dog around. Nobody had. One lady said she thought he was an angel dressed like a St. Bernard.

My mother said an angel must have sent him. She said if a real angel came to me out there in the woods, I might have been too scared. But if an angel sent a nice dog to lead me home, I would like that. Well, I sure did like it, and all my life I will believe in angels.[101]

67
Angel on a Bicycle

Gina and I were coming home from high school and it was pouring down rain to the point that we couldn't see in front of us. We were trying to find the safest way home, but after we turned left at the stop sign, we knew we were in trouble.

We were in the water and our car wouldn't move. Water began seeping in and soon it was covering the floormats. But we couldn't get out because the water pressure was too great to open our doors.

We knew the situation was beyond us so we bowed our heads in prayer. We asked God to please send us help. Then as we finished praying, we looked up to see a young man riding his bicycle in the middle of the street. We were almost afraid to open the window for fear water would come rushing in. But finally we dared it and he said, "My name is Dave and I came to help you." Then he gave us his hand and we climbed out the window.

We headed toward some apartments. These were the kind with a high fence and gate locked tight. While we were talking about how to get through the locked gate, Dave was suddenly on the other side turning the lock. Then he opened it for us and we walked through. But when we turned to thank him, he was gone. Vanished completely.

As long as we live, Gina and I will believe Dave was a real angel, an angel on a bicycle, sent to rescue us.[102]

68
An Angel of Cloud and Fire

"**I** am sending an angel ahead of you to guard you along the way and to bring you to the place I have prepared."

By day the Lord went ahead of them in a pillar of cloud to guide them on their way and by night in a pillar of fire to give them light, so that they could travel by day or night. Neither the pillar of cloud by day nor the pillar of fire by night left its place in front of the people.[103]

∞

Was the pillar-cloud an angel? Certainly it served as a sign of God's protective guidance. Likewise with the pillar of fire. No mere token symbols of God, these "pillars" were altogether supernatural, fearfully awe-inspiring, bigger than a silo... and *moving* to lead the way.

∞

"Our mother lay in a coma, dying. She had become a Christian during her long battle with cancer. Now the end was very near. It was my sister's turn to keep watch through the night in the living room where the hospital bed and all of the medical equipment occupied most of the space. She dozed off on a couch next to the bed.

"A small noise woke me up. I thought Mom needed me. Then I realized she couldn't summon me, because she was unconscious. But when I opened my eyes, I saw blue lights shimmering in the dark room like the aurora borealis. I was so surprised. I know what I saw, and I know it was angels, waiting with me, ready to take her home."[104]

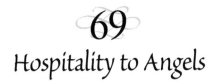

69
Hospitality to Angels

Abraham looked up and saw three men standing nearby. When he saw them, he hurried from the entrance of his tent to meet them and bowed low to the ground.

He said, "If I have found favor in your eyes,… do not pass your servant by. Let a little water be brought, and then you may all wash your feet and rest under this tree. Let me get you something to eat, so you can be refreshed and then go on your way—now that you have come to your servant."

"Very well," they answered, "do as you say."

So Abraham hurried into the tent to Sarah. "Quick," he said, "get three seahs of the fine flour and knead it and bake some bread."

Then he ran to the herd and selected a choice, tender calf and gave it to a servant, who hurried to prepare it. He then brought some curds and milk and the calf that had been prepared, and set these before them. While they ate, he stood near them under a tree.

∞

The two angels arrived at Sodom in the evening, and Lot was sitting in the gateway of the city. When he saw them, he got up to meet them and bowed down with his face to the ground. "My lords," he said, "please turn aside to your servant's house. You can wash your feet and spend the night and then go on your way early in the morning."

"No," they answered. "We will spend the night in the square."

But he insisted so strongly that they did go with him and entered his house.[105]

70
The Angel with the Scroll

Then I saw another mighty angel coming down from heaven, surrounded by a cloud, with a rainbow over his head; his face shone like the sun and his feet flashed with fire. And he held open in his hand a small scroll. He set his right foot on the sea and his left foot on the earth, and gave a great shout—it was like the roar of a lion—and the seven thunders crashed their reply.

I was about to write what the thunders said when a voice from heaven called to me, "Don't do it. Their words are not to be revealed."

Then the voice from heaven spoke to me again, "Go and get the unrolled scroll from the mighty angel standing there upon the sea and land."

So I approached him and asked him to give me the scroll. "Yes, take it and eat it," he said. "At first it will taste like honey, but when you swallow it, it will make your stomach sour!" So I took it from his hand, and ate it! And just as he had said, it was sweet in my mouth but it gave me a stomach ache when I swallowed it.

Then he told me, "You must prophesy further about many peoples, nations, tribes, and kings."[106]

71

Elisha and the Chariots of Fire

Dothan was just a small village in the middle of Israel. But the whole Syrian army converged upon it one night under cover of darkness. It was because of the prophet Elisha.

Somehow, the king of Israel had been able to anticipate even the most secret plot of the king of Syria. How could Syria ever win the war against Israel? The officers of the king of Syria, when he had accused them of harboring an informant, had told him about Elisha, the "secret weapon" of the king of Israel: "Elisha, the prophet, tells the king of Israel even the words you speak in the privacy of your bedroom!"

So after his spies confirmed Elisha's whereabouts in Dothan, the king of Syria sent his great army, complete with horses and chariots, to hem in the prophet in his city of refuge.

When the prophet's servant got up early the next morning and went outside, there were troops, horses, and chariots everywhere.

"Alas, my master, what shall we do?" he cried out to Elisha.

"Don't be afraid!" Elisha told him. "For our army is bigger than theirs!" Then Elisha prayed, "Lord, open his eyes and let him see!" And the Lord opened the young man's eyes so that he could see horses of fire and chariots of fire everywhere upon the mountain![107]

72
The Angel Who Liked to Fly

Several years ago, I was accompanying my husband on a free vacation he had won at work. Unfortunately, I was not at all happy about this wonderful opportunity to travel. You see, I was terrified of flying. In fact, I was so overcome by fear before the trip that I would not pack my suitcase until the day we left.

As the plane was lifting off the runway, I managed a quick glance out the window. There near the end of the wing of the plane was an angel! It was about the size of a seven- or eight-year-old child, and as far as I could tell, this angel did not have wings of its own!

He had a face, though, although it was not skinlike. His countenance was crystal white and bright with exuberance and happiness. He looked like he enjoyed flying! I felt such peace about our trip.

The angel remained on the wing for hours. When we began our descent over Florida, I saw the angel go straight up into the sky. Mission accomplished. No one else saw the angel, but no one could ever convince me that what I saw wasn't real.[108]

73

Heaven-Sent Protectors

He ordered his angels
to guard you wherever you go.
If you stumble, they'll catch you;
their job is to keep you from falling.[109]

∽

When I was desperate, I called out,
And God got me out of a tight spot.

God's angel sets up a circle
of protection around us while we pray.[110]

∽

Frustrate all those
who are plotting my downfall.
Make them like cinders in a high wind,
with God's angel working the bellows.
Make their road lightless and mud-slick,
with God's angel on their tails.[111]

74

An Angel Stops Balaam Cold

When Balaam's donkey saw the angel of the Lord standing in the road with a drawn sword in his hand, she turned off the road into a field. Balaam beat her to get her back on the road.

Then the angel of the Lord stood in a narrow path between two vineyards, with walls on both sides. When the donkey saw the angel of the Lord, she pressed close to the wall, crushing Balaam's foot against it. So he beat her again.

Then the angel of the Lord moved on ahead and stood in a narrow place where there was no room to turn, either to the right or to the left. When the donkey saw the angel of the Lord, she lay down under Balaam, and he was angry and beat her with his staff.

Then the Lord opened Balaam's eyes, and he saw the angel of the Lord standing in the road with his sword drawn. So he bowed low and fell facedown.

The angel of the Lord asked him, "Why have you beaten your donkey these three times? I have come here to oppose you because your path is a reckless one before me."[112]

75

When Angels Block Your Path

Balaam had prophetic gifts. That's why the king of Moab had summoned him. He wanted Balaam to place a curse on the Israelites who were encamped nearby. On his way to the king, Balaam encountered a fierce angel who blocked his path. His donkey saw the angel, though Balaam didn't. When the animal refused to budge, Balaam kept hitting the beast to get him to move. Then God opened his eyes and the angel spoke to him.

This story tells us that angels sometimes block our path because we are heading in the wrong direction.

Perhaps you are feeling thwarted in some way. You may be involved in a relationship that is going nowhere, a business deal that has soured, a ministry that is fraught with trouble. How do you know if you are under spiritual attack or if an angel of the Lord is trying to tell you something? Rather than assuming you know what God's will is, stop and ask him for wisdom. Pray that he will help you discern what is really going on. Is this a situation that calls for endurance and perseverance, or is God trying to point out another direction for you or your ministry?

Resist the temptation to keep beating your particular donkey, to force him to tread the path you have chosen. Ask humbly for God to guide you, and he will show you if one of his angels is blocking the path ahead. If he is, you dare not risk going forward.[113]

76

Look!

The trees reflected in the river—they are unconscious of a spiritual world so near them. So are we.[114]

∞

I suspect that the biggest reason why we don't know what an angel's physical being is like is because our internal sight is too limited. Jesus said, "Look! The kingdom of God is all around you, in your very midst." I have always felt that he meant that even though our human senses, physical and spiritual, aren't sensitive enough to see and know God directly, or even the angelic servants of God or those we love who have gone before us, nonetheless, what we call heaven and earth are separated by far less than we think. If our lives were utterly pure and filled with light and love, we would find no barrier between the dimension we live in and that of the angels. We would see them constantly. We would see the face of God unveiled, and it would consume and transform us totally and all around us. If we could only "Look!"[115]

∞

The soul should always stand ajar, ready to welcome the ecstatic experience.[116]

77

An Angel Visits Samson's Parents

One day the Angel of the Lord appeared to the wife of Manoah, of the tribe of Dan, who lived in the city of Zorah. She had no children, but the Angel said to her, "Even though you have been barren so long, you will soon conceive and have a son! Don't drink any wine or beer, and don't eat any food that isn't kosher. Your son's hair must never be cut, for he shall be a Nazirite, a special servant of God from the time of his birth; and he will begin to rescue Israel from the Philistines."

The woman ran and told her husband....Then Manoah prayed, "O Lord, please let the man from God come back to us again and give us more instructions about the child you are going to give us." The Lord answered his prayer, and the Angel of God appeared once again to his wife as she was sitting in the field. But again she was alone—Manoah was not with her—so she quickly ran and found her husband and told him, "The same man is here again!"

Manoah ran back with his wife and asked, "...Can you give us any special instructions about how we should raise the baby after he is born?"

And the Angel replied, "Be sure that your wife follows the instructions I gave her...."

Then Manoah said to the Angel, "Please stay here until we can get you something to eat."

"I'll stay," the Angel replied, "but I'll not eat anything. However, if you wish to bring something, bring an offering to sacrifice to the Lord."

Then Manoah asked him for his name. "When all this comes true and the baby is born," he said to the Angel, "we will certainly want to tell everyone that you predicted it!"

"Don't even ask my name," the Angel replied, "for it is a secret."

Then Manoah took a young goat and a grain offering and offered it as a sacrifice to the Lord; and the Angel did a strange and wonderful thing, for as the flames from the altar were leaping up toward the sky, and as Manoah and his wife watched, the Angel ascended in the fire![117]

78
Heavenly Soldiers

Corrie ten Boom liked to recount a happening during the Juenesse Rebellion in the Congo, when the rebels advanced on a school where two hundred children of missionaries lived. "They planned to kill both children and teachers," she writes. "In the school, they knew of the danger and therefore went to prayer. Their only protection was a fence and a couple of soldiers, while the enemy, who came closer and closer, amounted to several hundreds."

When the rebels were close by, suddenly something happened: They turned around and ran away! The same thing happened on the second and third day. One of the rebels was wounded and was brought to the missionary hospital. When the doctor was busy dressing his wounds, he asked him: "Why did you not break into the school as you planned?"

"We could not do it," the soldier said. "We saw hundreds of soldiers in white uniforms, and we became scared...."

"In Africa," Corrie explains, "soldiers never wear white uniforms. So it must have been angels. What a wonderful thing that the Lord can open the eyes of the enemy so that they see angels!"[118]

79
Bright Bird of God

See how he scorns to use man's instruments;
he needs no oars, no sails, only his wings
to navigate between such distant shores.

"See how he has them pointing up to Heaven:
he fans the air with these immortal plumes
that do not moult as mortal feathers do."

Closer and closer to our shore he came,
brighter and brighter shone the bird of God,
until I could no longer bear the light,

and bowed my head. He steered straight to the shore,
his boat so swift and light upon the wave,
it left no sign of truly sailing there;

and the celestial pilot stood astern
with blessedness inscribed upon his face.
More than a hundred souls were in his ship:

In exitu Israel de Aegypto,
they were all singing with a single voice,
chanting it verse by verse until the end.

The angel signed them with the holy cross,
and they rushed from the ship onto the shore;
he disappeared, swiftly, as he had come.[119]

80

An Angel Destroys an Army

King Sennacherib of Assyria mocked the Lord God and God's servant Hezekiah, heaping up insults. The king also sent letters scorning the Lord God of Israel.

"The gods of all the other nations failed to save their people from my hand, and the God of Hezekiah will fail, too," he wrote.

The messengers who brought the letters shouted threats to the people gathered on the walls of the city, trying to frighten and dishearten them. These messengers talked about the God of Jerusalem just as though he were one of the heathen gods—a handmade idol!

Then King Hezekiah and Isaiah the prophet cried out in prayer to God in heaven, and the Lord sent an angel who destroyed the Assyrian army with all its officers and generals! So Sennacherib returned home in deep shame to his own land.

That is how the Lord saved Hezekiah and the people of Jerusalem. And now there was peace at last throughout his realm.[120]

∞

Immediately, because Herod did not give praise to God, an angel of the Lord struck him down, and he was eaten by worms and died.[121]

81
Think of It!

The high priest and all his associates, who were members of the party of the Sadducees, were filled with jealousy. They arrested the apostles and put them in the public jail. But during the night an angel of the Lord opened the doors of the jail and brought them out. "Go, stand in the temple courts," he said, "and tell the people the full message of this new life."

At daybreak they entered the temple courts, as they had been told, and began to teach the people.[122]

∞

Think of it! Whether we see them or not, God has created a vast host of angels to help accomplish his work in this world. When we know God personally through faith in his Son, Jesus Christ, we can have confidence that the angels of God will watch over us and assist us because we belong to him.[123]

82
Our Angels Understand Our Needs

We are like children, who stand in need of masters to enlighten us and direct us; and God has provided for this, by appointing his angels to be our teachers and guides.[124]

∞

It may seem that our life journey—the path chosen for us by God—is much too difficult, even if we do have angels to escort us on our way. After all, we still have to be the ones who suffer.

How very true! And each of our guardian angels is keenly aware of it. But this IS the very *reason* they work so hard, behind the scenes, trying to take our eyes off the problem below and up to the only adequate answer above: *Jesus, our suffering Master, our risen Lord*.

While we are on the journey, he pairs us up with our angel. If we only lift our eyes to the invisible realm of the spirit, we will become aware that we truly *are* guarded and guided. We will be consoled, and taught, day by day, to advance in virtue.

As a dim awareness of our angel grows stronger and stronger, we will know that our friendship is not based on emotion but on the only thing that will never change, and never end: our joint love for the living God.[125]

83

Angels Show Us the Way
Even Before We Ask

When suddenly closed eyes are struck by light,
our sleep is broken, though it lingers on
a little while before it fully dies,

just so my vision slipped away from me
when I was struck by light across my eyes,
a light far brighter than is known on earth.

Looking around to find out where I was,
I heard a voice: "Here is the place to climb."
This drove all other thoughts out of my mind

and left me burning with desire to see
the one who spoke—a wish that will not cease
till it comes face-to-face with its desire;

but, as if looking at the burning sun
whose brilliance overwhelms the sight and veils
its very form, I felt my powers fail.

"This is an angel of the Lord who comes
to show us the ascent before we ask,
and hides himself in his own radiance.

"He treats us as a man would treat himself:
who sees the need but waits for the request,
already is half-guilty of denial;

"So, let our feet obey his call, and climb
as far as possible while there is light,
for we may not ascend once it grows dark."[126]

84

Two Flew Over the Handlebars

Joyce Brown was riding her bicycle, coming home from work in the late afternoon. The Arizona sun was low on the horizon, making visibility difficult for everyone on the street. Joyce pedaled to the intersection, where there was a stop sign. Instead of making a complete stop, she eased around the corner and was hit from behind by a truck whose driver did not see her. Joyce flew over the handlebars. Although she was not a Christian, she cried out, "Jesus! Help me!"

Immediately Joyce felt herself being cushioned, as though she were wrapped in pillows. When she landed, witnesses said she bounced like a person landing on a trampoline. Joyce felt no pain. As a precaution she went to the hospital, where a thorough check revealed no serious injuries. Ask Joyce for an explanation, and she will tell you that those pillows were angels gently carrying her. In gratitude, Joyce began a spiritual quest that brought her to faith in the same Jesus who had answered her emergency prayer.[127]

85

Two Strong Arms

Jean Blitz was expecting her fifth child in a few months. On a cold spring morning she awakened in her Wichita home early and, after making the coffee, went outside to see if the milkman had made his delivery.

During the night the back porch had become glazed with ice, and as Jean stepped onto it, both her feet slipped out from under her. There was no railing on the stoop, nowhere to catch hold and keep herself from tumbling down the stairs. Almost in slow motion, Jean saw herself falling... falling... perhaps losing her unborn baby.

Then all of a sudden, two strong arms caught Jean and stood her up straight against the door. Thank heaven her husband had awakened early and was at the right place at the right time! Her grateful heart still pounding, she turned to him... but there was no one there at all. The door stood open, the kitchen beyond was empty, and even the snow-covered yard was silent, except for a little sigh in the wind.

Jean's baby was born strong and healthy, and today is the father of eight.[128]

86
The Blustery Day

Can angels rescue us even when we never see them?

On a very stormy and blustery morning, seventy-nine-year-old Anna May Arthur was climbing the steep steps of a cathedral in her native Ireland.

As she climbed, the wind buffeted her and she felt unsteady and vulnerable. As she approached the top, an especially strong gust caught her and she started to tumble backward.

Instinctively Anna May appealed to heaven, crying, "Oh, my guardian angel, save me!" Immediately she felt two strong hands on her back, pushing her forward and erect.

"I really wasn't surprised," Anna May says. "In fact, it crossed my mind that when I turned, I would actually see a heavenly being in white!"

But when Anna May turned, she saw a neighbor holding her upright. She had known Thomas Hillen for years, and was aware that he suffered with very bad heart trouble. Because of his debilitating illness, Thomas always walked at a snail's pace.

"Thomas, how did you get up here so fast?"

"I don't know!" His face was bewildered. He had been at the church gate, at least forty paces from the bottom step, when he saw Anna May lose her balance at the top of the flight.

And suddenly *he* was there too, across the courtyard and up the steps, right behind her. "I don't remember crossing the distance. I—I seem to have been carried," Thomas told her.[129]

87

An Angelic Magic Trick

On a gloomy day years ago, my sister and I were driving back home on the old Columbia River Highway. As we went past the beautiful Multnomah Falls near Larch Mountain, Elva said suddenly, "How odd. Why is that woman sitting there with an umbrella? It isn't raining."

"What woman?" I said. I had seen no one. I thought Elva must have dozed off and dreamed it.

"She was sitting on the ground beside the road," Elva insisted.

At home, we heard on TV that two hikers were lost on Larch Mountain. "I'm *sure* I saw one of those women," Elva kept saying, until finally we called the sheriff's office. Two officers asked us to drive with them to the place where Elva had seen the woman. Sheriff Terry Schrunk said that Elva's description jibed perfectly with one of the women, even to the umbrella and the color of her clothes. The police searched into the darkness, then said they'd continue in the morning.

At 10:00 A.M., Sheriff Schrunk called—the women had been found! "They were on the mountain right above where your sister said we should look," he told me. "They were trapped above the falls."

"Trapped"—the women had been trapped, he said. They couldn't climb down. That meant there was no way that Elva could have seen one of them sitting beside the highway![130]

88
Beggars Indeed!

St. Francis of Assisi, well-known to this day, held dearly the triple virtues of poverty, chastity, and obedience.

One spring, when he was ill and near the end of his life, some of his caretakers had Francis taken to Siena, where some physicians of good reputation lived. During this journey in the plain extending south of San Quirico d'Orcia, a meeting occurred that has become legendary.

Francis saw three old women coming toward him, so perfectly alike in age, height, and features that one would have thought them triplets. As they passed him, they bowed reverently and greeted him.... Believing them to be beggar women, he requested the doctor who accompanied him to give them something. Dismounting, the latter gave each of them some money. Thereupon the three sisters disappeared so suddenly that the travelers, who had turned around almost at once, were unable to see what had become of them. "It was doubtless a celestial vision," wrote St. Bonaventure later, "symbolic of the virtues of poverty, chastity, and obedience, to which Francis had always been so faithful." [131]

A Little-Known Christmas Eve Story

"Gabby, you know all about the invasion plans, don't you?"

"No, Mike. No one knows *all* about them. You know how Army Intelligence works."

"Well, listen up. I have three secrets for you: First, the invasion is tomorrow night. Second, the place—It's a little town no one would ever suspect. Third, the identity of our new spy. She's a woman."

"A woman! Why?"

"Mike, don't be such an old chauvinist. This one's perfect for the job, just perfect. She's been preparing the landing place now for months."

"How do you know all this?"

"I was the one that got the first message through. I had to wait for her reply; the General absolutely insisted that we wait until we got her permission."

"Permission? The General waited for the permission of a woman before the great invasion could happen? Incredible! If I didn't know better, I'd swear the General had lost his marbles."

"You haven't heard the half of it. Hold on to your hat for this one, Mike. The General insisted on personally leading the invasion, not just directing it from across the Channel. He's already there, in disguise. He landed nine months ago."

"This is horribly dangerous, Gabby. Suppose he is captured? What a plum *that* would be for the enemy…. By the way, how many troops are in the invasion forces? If you're leading them tomorrow, you must know."

"You wouldn't believe it. The world has never seen an army this big. The whole sky is gonna have to open up for this one."[132]

90
Irish Cottage Angels

She started the day by splashing her face with three palmfuls of water in the name of the Trinity. Then she made her bed.

> I make this bed
> In the name of the Father, the Son and the Holy Ghost,...
> In the name of each night, each day,
> Each angel that is in the heavens.

And now, at daybreak, before the rest of her family is awake, she starts to do what is her morning chore, to stir into life the fire banked down the night before. Fire was never taken for granted. It was seen as one of the miraculous gifts of God, given so that people have warmth and light, and it was for them at the same time a continual reminder that they too needed constant renewal. The lifting of the peats that brought the flame of the fire to life again was a daily task, done year in, year out. Yet by her words and gestures this woman gives it meaning.

> I will kindle my fire this morning
> In the presence of the holy angels of heaven....
> God kindle thou in my heart within
> A flame of love to my neighbor,
> To my foe, to my friend, to my kindred all...

To the brave, to the knave, to the thrall...
Without malice, without jealousy, without envy
Without fear, without terror of anyone under the sun.
From the lowliest thing that liveth
To the Name that is highest of all.

The day would end with the "smooring" or smothering of the fire, and again this would be done with a ritual which involved the laying down of the peats in the name of the Trinity and the saints and the angels.[133]

91
Angel in the Corral

Jared knew what he had seen. He had watched helplessly as his wife's horse pitched her off—fearful as he saw her foot still caught in the stirrup. He expected the horse to drag her violently across the rough rocks, but as soon as she was dethroned from the saddle, Jared saw everything change into slow motion. As an accomplished horseman, Jared knew that horses do not buck slowly, thus he watched in amazement as he saw his wife almost float to the ground, with one deft movement freeing her foot from the stirrup.

Ask Margy today what she believes, and she will answer with confidence: "Angels *are*. They do exist. They continue to do their work with ease, agility, and a preciseness that defies even the law of gravity when necessary. My own guardian angel? Yes, you had better believe it. For myself, there was absolutely no room for doubt. I had no option but to believe it. I am so thankful for that experience—an experience that didn't break my back but only opened my eyes."[134]

"Your Child Is Safe"

It was late morning in a picturesque little French village, blessedly quiet and peaceful after the years of World War II bloodshed and violence. The Americans were there only as occupation troops to help rebuild; among them was a young surgeon who was responsible for setting up a hospital.

His wife and son—just a toddler—were at their home, which was on five acres of land, much of it uncleared. A ravine was at one end, with high trees and brush, and there was even an old, deep well on the property.

"Charlie, come home!" the young mother called on the phone in desperation. "Stephen is lost! I can't find him!"

Without another word, she ran outside, thinking that Stephen might have fallen down the well.

"Oh, my God! Is that his red sweater down there?" she screamed as she peered down into the damp darkness.

Suddenly, an army truck roared in the distance and she spun around, knowing her husband was bringing some soldiers from the base to help with the search. But no need! There was Stephen, right before her, little Stephen and a most unusual man, who simply held his hand.

"Do not be afraid," said the man in an incredibly kind and understanding voice. "Your child is safe."

In joy and relief she scooped up her little boy. When she looked up to thank his rescuer, he was gone![135]

93
Divine Paralysis?

It was early evening—a fatiguing and frustrating period of the day for all mothers—and Emily was preparing dinner. Diana, her toddler, was riding her toy horse around the kitchen. Several times Emily almost tripped over Diana and her clackety toy. Emily's patience was wearing thinner by the minute. Finally, in exasperation, she reached down to give the horse a hard push, to roll her daughter away from her.

"Suddenly I felt my whole arm stop in midair, like some sort of invisible block," Emily says. "I didn't feel another hand or a grip, but actual paralysis, which extended from my shoulder all the way down the upper extremity. I was aware that the power (or lack of it) was coming from something outside myself." Nor did her arm fall "asleep" or tingly; she could move it anywhere *except* toward Diana's horse.

Emily looked up, bewildered. And in one of those microseconds that seems eternal, she realized that the cellar door was open. Had she pushed Diana, the little girl would have shot across the floor, through the door—and down the steps to the stone floor below.[136]

94
Signposts of Hope

The angels in our midst are signposts of hope that our transformation—and that of the whole world—is possible. *Heaven is not a galaxy away,* they say; *it's here; the kingdom of God is here, in your very midst—and here we are to prove it. The barriers are not insuperable. Your problems are not insoluble. God is as near as your heartbeat.*[137]

∞

The Lord ministers to our weakness. I remember, on one of my visits to Chicago, feeling very much alone and threatened. People were jostling me on the sidewalk—so many of them going in both directions and headed for so many different destinations. There were people whizzing by in cars too, and I could hear the rumble of the elevated trains overhead, carrying another crowd of persons to a whole variety of places. Not far from where I stood was a busy airport filled with people taking off and landing.

As I stood there in that crowded place, I found myself wondering, Can God really take personal care of me and at the same time take care of all the believers on the sidewalk and in the cars and on the trains and in the airplanes? What about my wife and children in Michigan, my parents and siblings in Iowa, and my aunt in California?

Then I thought of God's angels. His myriad of angels, ten thousand times ten thousand and thousands of thousands more. Somehow "I will never leave you nor forsake you" was easier to accept and understand when I thought of God's angels all around me. [138]

95

"They Came to Take Her to Jesus"

Katherine was born weighing all of one pound, nine ounces and was quickly rushed off to the neonatal unit. We were so happy she was alive. And there was hope—hope for a miracle.

A week after her birth, as I walked to the neonatal unit, I thought of my tiny baby and long fight that was ahead of her. I reached the special care unit and pulled on the required gown. Pushing up my sleeves to perform the obligatory fingers-to-elbow scrubbing, I turned to look through the large glass window to see Katherine lying in her incubator.

Suddenly I stopped motionless over the basin, transfixed at the sight of two very large figures standing on either side of her incubator. They had to be at least ten feet tall, with very large shoulders. And they shined with the brightest white light I had ever seen. I knew they were angels and I was certain they were there to protect my daughter.

By the next day, Katherine was gone. I began to question the Lord: "Why did you send those angels? I thought they were there to protect my daughter, to keep her safe as she grew."

I'm sure it was no coincidence that my wife and I just happened to watch Billy Graham on television about two weeks later. The believer, he declared, is never out of the Lord's care. Even at our death, he provides angels to usher us into his presence. Yes, the angels that visited Katherine's incubator had a mission, but it was not just to protect her. More importantly, they came to take her to Jesus.[139]

96

"Can't You See the Angels?"

Joann Kruse's cousin suffered from leukemia as a young child. "Poor Catherine was frightened of dying, and my aunt and uncle didn't know what to say to comfort her. Finally, a family friend began to talk to her about God and his angels. He told Catherine that God loved her very much, so much so that he had provided angels to watch over her. When the time came for her to make the journey to heaven, the angels would be there to keep her safe, he told her.

"I remember the year Catherine turned ten. It was the beginning of the end. She became so weak that she couldn't even sit up in bed anymore. While my aunt and uncle were keeping vigil one afternoon by her bedside, she shocked them by suddenly sitting straight up and pointing. 'Can't you see the angels? They're all around us!' she said excitedly.

"Uncle Ray asked her what the angels were doing. 'They're laughing and one of them is stretching out his arms and asking me if I would like to go with them,' the little girl replied.

"'Would you like to go?' my uncle asked.

"'If it's all right with you and Mom,' she replied. It must have broken their hearts, but both parents nodded their assent, and Catherine stretched out her small arms, reaching toward invisible hands. The very next instant, she was gone."[140]

97

Angelic Doormen

Just as an angel was involved in Christ's resurrection, so will angels help us in death. Only one thin veil separates our natural world from the spiritual world. That thin veil we call death. However, Christ both vanquished death and overcame the dark threats of the evil fallen angels. So now God surrounds death with the assurance of angelic help to bring pulsing life out of the darkness of that experience for believers. We inherit the kingdom of God.[141]

Angels appear on the edge of death because death is the threshold between time and eternity. Death is a room with a view beyond the veil. In the Bible, nearly every encounter with heaven—visions, dreams, miracles, revelations about the future, the Second Coming of Christ, and the Day of Judgment—is enveloped in the presence of angels. If death is the door to eternity, angels are doormen. They were, in fact, the gatekeepers at the empty tomb of the Savior! Angels were all around, witnessing the resurrection and announcing it to his disciples.[142]

98

Angels Announce Jesus' Resurrection

After the Sabbath, as the first light of the new week dawned, Mary Magdalene and the other Mary went to keep vigil at the tomb.

Suddenly the earth reeled and rocked under their feet as God's angel came down from heaven, came right up to where they were standing. He rolled back the stone and then sat on it. Shafts of lightning blazed from him. His garments shimmered snow-white. The guards at the tomb were scared to death. They were so frightened, they couldn't move.

The angel spoke to the women: "There is nothing to fear here. I know you're looking for Jesus, the One they nailed to the cross. He is not here. He was raised, just as he said. Come and look at the place where he was placed.

"Now, get on your way quickly and tell his disciples, 'He is risen from the dead. He is going on ahead of you to Galilee. You will see him there.' That's the message."

The women, deep in wonder and full of joy, lost no time in leaving the tomb. They ran to tell the disciples. Then Jesus met them, stopping them in their tracks. "Good morning!" he said. They fell to their knees, embraced his feet, and worshiped him. Jesus said, "You're holding on to me for dear life! Don't be frightened like that. Go tell my brothers that they are to go to Galilee, and that I'll meet them there."[143]

99

Safe Passage

In telling the story in Luke 16, Jesus says that the beggar was "carried by the angels." He was not only escorted; he was *carried*. What an experience that must have been for Lazarus! He had lain begging at the gate of the rich man until his death, but then suddenly he found himself carried by the mighty angels of God!

Once I stood in London to watch Queen Elizabeth return from an overseas trip. I saw the parade of dignitaries, the marching bands, the crack troops, the waving flags. I saw all the splendor that accompanies the homecoming of a queen. However, that was nothing compared to the homecoming of a true believer who has said goodbye here to all of the suffering of this life and been immediately surrounded by angels who carry him upward to the glorious welcome awaiting the redeemed in heaven.

The Christian should never consider death a tragedy. Rather he should see it as angels do: They realize that joy should mark the journey from time to eternity. The way to life is by the valley of death, but the road is marked with victory all the way. Angels revel in the power of the resurrection of Jesus, which assures us of our resurrection and guarantees us a safe passage to heaven.[144]

100
A Blessed Peace of Mind

It was exactly one year since her husband Chris had been diagnosed with acute lymphocytic leukemia, but the last months had been particularly difficult for forty-year-old Melissa—gruesome treatments brought only sleepless nights and no hope.

Utter exhaustion finally overpowered her as she kept her usual vigil near Chris' bed. Then at three in the morning a frantic nurse shook her awake, telling her that her husband was missing.

Melissa was instantly up and running, determined to find him. When she glanced toward the chapel, she could see two figures, one of them Chris. She burst in, demanding to know where he'd been and whether he was all right.

"I'm all right," Chris said, smiling.

His companion—a tall, ageless-looking man, casually but neatly dressed—remained quietly unobtrusive. Melissa was struck by his smooth pale skin and ice-blue eyes. She also gathered that Chris wanted to be left alone.

When Chris returned to his room some time later, he no longer looked like a weak, terminally ill man. He "was lit up, just vibrant," and told Melissa the man with him in the chapel was his guardian angel.

There was no more fear. No more pain. Only a blessed peace of mind, even though the cancer was not cured. Two days later, Chris died with his prayers answered.

"I know what I saw," Melissa says a dozen years later. "Never, never, never will anyone be able to convince me that angels don't exist."[145]

101
"I've Been with the Angels!"

Wayne Herring is a Presbyterian pastor in Memphis, Tennessee, who knows that angels sometimes show up just when we need them most.

"My aunt, Kate Lewis, loved Christ all her life. She and my uncle had no children of their own, and my aunt treated me like her own son.

"Five years ago my aunt lay dying of congestive heart failure. In her late eighties, her frail body was no match for the disease. Her struggle with death was prolonged and agonizing. She was gasping for breath and had been semi-comatose for many days. At one point the nurses actually tried to revive her by initiating some heroic measures to prolong her life. My father was at my aunt's bedside when it happened. Suddenly Aunt Kate sat straight up and looked around at everyone in the room. Her eyes were sharp and her speech clear, but she wasn't happy. 'Why on earth did you bring me back?' she scolded. 'It's been wonderful. I've been with the angels and I didn't want to leave!' These were her last words. She sank back down on her pillow, and a few days later she was gone."[146]

102

"The Angel Came to Get Mommy"

Gilbert Axton's wife, Ethel, and his nine-year-old daughter, Maribel, were killed in an automobile accident in Bloomington, Indiana, and his six-year-old daughter, Sheri, was severely injured.

"In my deep sorrow, I had no idea how I was going to break the news to Sheri that her mother and her sister were dead," Axton said. "I stood outside her hospital room for several minutes, praying for guidance."

Steeling himself to the awful task at hand, Gilbert Axton entered his daughter's hospital room, trying his best to fight back the tears that spilled down his cheeks.

But before he could break the news to Sheri, she told him that she already knew about the death of her mother and sister.

"While I was lying on the ground beside the car, I saw a beautiful angel come to get Mommy," she said. "The angel started to go back to the sky with Mommy, but then he stopped. He came back to the ground and stood over Maribel for a little bit, like he was trying to make up his mind. And then he took Maribel by the hand, too, and took both of them with him to heaven."[147]

103
Why Angels Don't Always Help Us

Why do guardian angels intervene for some saints like Peter, and not others like James? Why do guardian angels save some children and not others? Why do guardian angels prevent some car accidents and not others? What good is a bodyguard if he doesn't guard your body all the time?

We don't know the whole answer to that question. We *do* know, however, that the kingdom of God is at hand, but it hasn't fully come. What God does for us in this life is just an appetizer. We're still waiting for the full meal.

At present not everything is the way we would like it. Not everything is subject to us, even though we are just a little lower than the angels.

This is the tension between what some call the "now" and the "not yet," between "what is" and "what ought to be." For whatever unexplained heavenly reasons, there are many times when God chooses to intervene directly in our lives—*now*. Other times, neither he nor his guardian angels steps in to rescue us. Those are the moments when the kingdom of God has *not yet* fully come. We might even start wondering if there is a God. Or if there is, does he care? Maybe God isn't all-loving, we think.

Why would the angel that saved Peter stand at a distance and watch James be put to death with the sword? We're not exactly sure. And yet, we have to be profoundly grateful for the angel who opened Peter's prison. And for all the angels who have helped and saved numberless saints and sinners through the centuries. Including us.[148]

104
Good and Bad Angels

Satan himself masquerades as an angel of light.[149]

∞

The word "angelic" usually has the connotation of perfect moral goodness, but that must not lead us to forget that the demons are angelic in their nature although of a diabolical or evil will.[150]

∞

The good and bad angels have arisen, not from a difference in their nature and origin but from a difference in their wills and desires. While some steadfastly continued in that which was the common good of all, namely, in God himself, and in his eternity, truth, and love; others became proud, deceived, envious.[151]

∞

The true cause of the blessedness of the good angels is found to be this, that they cleave to him who supremely is. And if we ask the cause of the misery of the bad, it occurs to us, and not unreasonably, that they are miserable because they have forsaken him who supremely is and have turned to themselves who have no such essence. And this vice, what else is it called than pride? For "pride is the beginning of sin."[152]

105
Angelic Destiny

In the first moment of angelic existence, as St. Augustine imagined it, the most perfect of God's creatures turned inward and discovered both itself and its Creator. For the angel, to know itself was to perceive within its being a dim reflection of God, mirrored darkly in his handiwork, and this obscure perception, which the tradition called the "twilight vision," was testimony of the link that bound the angel to its Maker. Thereafter, some of the angels turned to reality above them, to await the eternal morning of vision face-to-face, while others remained within themselves, and sank into eternal night. In those two moments, angelic destiny was fulfilled, and the light was separated from the darkness.

This separation left no room for a middle ground. Twilight, like indecision, is a temporal condition, and ceases to exist at the moment of choice. The human being may struggle throughout life in the hazy province of neither/nor, but the angels had only a moment in which to deliberate, and, once committed, were fixed for eternity.[153]

106

Angelic Power versus Demonic Power

The devil is an angel too.[154]

∞

The wars among nations on earth are merely popgun affairs compared to the fierceness of the battle in the spiritual unseen world.[155]

∞

And I saw an angel coming down out of heaven, having the key to the Abyss and holding in his hand a great chain. He seized the dragon, that ancient serpent, who is the devil, or Satan, and bound him for a thousand years. He threw him into the Abyss, and locked and sealed it over him, to keep him from deceiving the nations anymore until the thousand years were ended.[156]

∞

Christians must never fail to sense the operation of angelic glory. It forever eclipses the world of demonic powers, as the sun does the candle's light.[157]

107
Angels Help Us in Spiritual Battle

When we cried out to the Lord, he heard our cry and sent an angel and brought us out of Egypt.[158]

∞

One of Satan's sly devices is to divert our minds from the help God offers us in our struggles against the forces of evil. However, the Bible testifies that God has provided assistance for us in our spiritual conflicts. We are not alone in this world! The Bible teaches us that God's Holy Spirit has been given to empower us and guide us. In addition, the Bible—in nearly three hundred different places—also teaches that God has countless angels at his command. Furthermore, God has commissioned these angels to aid his children in their struggles against Satan.[159]

∞

God uses angels to work out the destinies of men and nations. He has altered the courses of the busy political and social arenas of our society and directed the destinies of men by angelic visitation many times over. We must be aware that angels keep in close and vital contact with all that is happening on the earth. Their knowledge of earthly matters exceeds that of men. We must attest to their invisible presence and unceasing labors. Let us believe that they are here among us. They may not laugh or cry with us, but we do know they delight with us over every victory in our evangelistic endeavors. Jesus taught that "there is joy in the presence of the angels of God when one sinner repents."[160]

108
The Angel of the Lord Honors Abraham

When they reached the place God had told him about, Abraham built an altar there and arranged the wood on it. He bound his son Isaac and laid him on the altar, on top of the wood. Then he reached out his hand and took the knife to slay his son. But the angel of the Lord called out to him from heaven, "Abraham! Abraham!"

"Here I am," he replied.

"Do not lay a hand on the boy," he said. "Do not do anything to him. Now I know that you fear God, because you have not withheld from me your son, your only son."

Abraham looked up and there in a thicket he saw a ram caught by its horns. He went over and took the ram and sacrificed it as a burnt offering instead of his son.

The angel of the Lord called to Abraham from heaven a second time and said, "I swear by myself, declares the Lord, that because you have done this and have not withheld your son, your only son, I will surely bless you and make your descendants as numerous as the stars in the sky and as the sand on the seashore. Your descendants will take possession of the cities of their enemies, and through your offspring all nations on earth will be blessed, because you have obeyed me."[161]

109
An Angel with a Sword

A nd God sent an angel to destroy Jerusalem. But as the angel was doing so, the Lord saw it and was grieved because of the calamity and said to the angel who was destroying the people, "Enough! Withdraw your hand."

David looked up and saw the angel of the Lord standing between heaven and earth, with a drawn sword in his hand extended over Jerusalem. Then David and the elders, clothed in sackcloth, fell face-down.

David said to God, "I am the one who has sinned and done wrong. These are but sheep. What have they done? O Lord my God, let your hand fall upon me and my family, but do not let this plague remain on your people."

Then the angel of the Lord ordered Gad to tell David to go up and build an altar to the Lord on the threshing floor of Araunah the Jebusite. So David went up in obedience to the word that Gad had spoken in the name of the Lord.

David built an altar to the Lord there and sacrificed burnt offerings and fellowship offerings. He called on the Lord, and the Lord answered him with fire from heaven on the altar of burnt offering.

Then the Lord spoke to the angel, and he put his sword back into its sheath.[162]

110

Angels Minister to Jesus

Then Jesus was led by the Spirit into the desert to be tempted by the devil. After fasting forty days and forty nights, he was hungry. The tempter came to him and said, "If you are the Son of God, tell these stones to become bread."

Jesus answered, "It is written: 'Man does not live on bread alone, but on every word that comes from the mouth of God.'"

Then the devil took him to the holy city and had him stand on the highest point of the temple. "If you are the Son of God," he said, "throw yourself down. For it is written: 'He will command his angels concerning you, and they will lift you up in their hands, so that you will not strike your foot against a stone.'"

Jesus answered him, "It is also written: 'Do not put the Lord your God to the test.'"

Again, the devil took him to a very high mountain and showed him all the kingdoms of the world and their splendor. "All this I will give you," he said, "if you will bow down and worship me."

Jesus said to him, "Away from me, Satan! For it is written: 'Worship the Lord your God, and serve him only.'"

Then the devil left him, and angels came and attended him.[163]

111

Angels in Your Wilderness

Jesus didn't decide on his own that it was time to take on the devil, but he allowed the Holy Spirit to initiate a season in his life in which he would endure testing and temptation. Moreover, the angels didn't appear on the scene until Jesus had successfully resisted every trick Satan threw at him. Only then did the heavenly host come and wait on him, much like a prizefighter's attendants after a fight.

At times, the Spirit will also lead us into the wilderness to endure a time of trial. It may be a wilderness of loneliness, illness, misunderstanding, poverty, failure, or doubt. Whatever the case, we can take courage from this crucial episode in Jesus' life.

There will be an end to your wilderness, a time when the angels will come and wait upon you as they did upon Jesus. That will be a time of rejoicing, a time of moving once again in power and confidence, a time of blessing as God continues to fulfill his purpose for your life.[164]

112
Jesus: Ruler of Angels and Demons

It is clear that the demons had great knowledge, and no charity. They feared Jesus' power to punish, and did not love his righteousness. He made known to them so much as he pleased, but he made himself known not as to the holy angels, who know him as the Word of God, and rejoice in his eternity, which they partake, but as was requisite to strike with terror the beings from whose tyranny he was going to free those who were predestined to his kingdom and the glory of it, eternally true and truly eternal. He made himself known, therefore, to the demons, not by that which is life eternal and unchangeable light which illumines the pious, whose souls are cleansed by faith in him, but by some temporal effects of his power and evidences of his mysterious presence. But when he judged it advisable gradually to suppress these signs and to retire into deeper obscurity, the prince of the demons doubted whether he were the Christ and endeavored to ascertain this by tempting him, insofar as he permitted himself to be tempted, that he might adapt the manhood he wore to be an example for our imitation. But after that temptation, when, as Scripture says, he was ministered to by the angels who are good and holy, and therefore objects of terror to the impure spirits, he revealed more and more distinctly to the demons how great he was, so that, even though the infirmity of his flesh might seem contemptible, none dared to resist his authority.[165]

113
Hurled from Heaven

I saw, on one side, him who was supposed
to be the noblest creature of creation,
plunge swift as lightning from the height of heaven.[166]

∞

And there was war in heaven. Michael and his angels fought against the dragon, and the dragon and his angels fought back. But he was not strong enough, and they lost their place in heaven. The great dragon was hurled down—that ancient serpent called the devil, or Satan, who leads the whole world astray. He was hurled to the earth, and his angels with him.

Then I heard a loud voice in heaven say: "Now have come the salvation and the power and the kingdom of our God, and the authority of his Christ. For the accuser of our brothers, who accuses them before our God day and night, has been hurled down. They overcame him by the blood of the Lamb and by the word of their testimony; they did not love their lives so much as to shrink from death. Therefore rejoice, you heavens and you who dwell in them! But woe to the earth and the sea, because the devil has gone down to you! He is filled with fury, because he knows that his time is short."[167]

114

Angels of Judgment and Destruction

The destroying angel cannot cross our threshold, because our doorposts are marked with the blood of the Lamb and the sign of the cross.[168]

∞

In his book *But That I Can't Believe*, John A.T. Robinson gives an interesting account of what we might call the "emasculation" of angels within the church and in popular thinking. He says that already in the theology of the Middle Ages angels were treated more like an intellectual puzzle than like a serious piece of theology.

Later in the Renaissance, Robinson claims, angels became domesticated, appearing as cherubs—sweet little boys with wings, whose blissful smiles bear little resemblance to their counterparts on earth. Then, during the Romantic movement, angels were sentimentalized as sexless creatures floating through pre-Raphaelite paintings and stained-glass windows.

It certainly is true that in popular thinking angels have become much less virile, less powerful, and more effeminate than what the Bible suggests. In the Bible, angels are consistently represented as male and are always referred to with masculine pronouns. And sometimes (as in the Book of Revelation) angels are presented as big and powerful. Moreover, the Bible presents angels as stout defenders of God's cause: legions of Michael's army routing the forces of Satan and his army, agents standing behind God's "law and order."[169]

115
God's Avenging Angels

The Bible says that throughout history angels have worked to carry out God's judgments, directing the destinies of nations disobedient to God. The writer of Hebrews speaks of angelic forces as executors of God's judgments: "Who maketh his angels spirits, and his ministers a flame of fire" (Hebrews 1:7). The flaming fire suggests how awful are the judgments of God and how burning is the power of the angels to carry out God's decisions. Angels administer judgment in accord with God's principles of righteousness. We often get false notions about angels from plays given by Sunday school children at Christmas. It is true that angels are ministering spirits sent to help the heirs of salvation. But just as they fulfill God's will in salvation for believers in Jesus Christ, so they are also "avengers" who use their great power to fulfill God's will in judgment. God has empowered them to separate the sheep from the goats, the wheat from the chaff, and one of them will blow the trumpet that announces impending judgment when God summons the nations to stand before him in the last great judgment.[170]

116
The Second Coming

"The sign of the Son of Man will appear in the sky, and all the nations of the earth will mourn. They will see the Son of Man coming on the clouds of the sky, with power and great glory. And he will send his angels with a loud trumpet call, and they will gather his elect from the four winds, from one end of the heavens to the other."

"When the Son of Man comes in his glory, and all the angels with him, he will sit on his throne in heavenly glory. All the nations will be gathered before him, and he will separate the people one from another as a shepherd separates the sheep from the goats. He will put the sheep on his right and the goats on his left.

"Then the King will say to those on his right, 'Come, you who are blessed by my Father; take your inheritance, the kingdom prepared for you since the creation of the world.

"Then he will say to those on his left, 'Depart from me, you who are cursed, into the eternal fire prepared for the devil and his angels.'"[171]

117

Angels Will Separate
the Wicked from the Righteous

His disciples came to him and said, "Explain to us the parable of the weeds in the field."

He answered, "The one who sowed the good seed is the Son of Man. The field is the world, and the good seed stands for the sons of the kingdom. The weeds are the sons of the evil one, and the enemy who sows them is the devil. The harvest is the end of the age, and the harvesters are angels.

"As the weeds are pulled up and burned in the fire, so it will be at the end of the age. The Son of Man will send out his angels, and they will weed out of his kingdom everything that causes sin and all who do evil. They will throw them into the fiery furnace, where there will be weeping and gnashing of teeth. Then the righteous will shine like the sun in the kingdom of their Father.

"The kingdom of heaven is like a net that was let down into the lake and caught all kinds of fish. When it was full, the fishermen pulled it up on the shore. Then they sat down and collected the good fish in baskets, but threw the bad away. This is how it will be at the end of the age. The angels will come and separate the wicked from the righteous and throw them into the fiery furnace."[172]

118

Three Angelic Prophecies for the Last Days

Then I saw another angel flying in midair, and he had the eternal gospel to proclaim to those who live on the earth—to every nation, tribe, language, and people. He said in a loud voice, "Fear God and give him glory, because the hour of his judgment has come. Worship him who made the heavens, the earth, the sea, and the springs of water."

A second angel followed and said, "Fallen! Fallen is Babylon the Great, which made all the nations drink the maddening wine of her adulteries."

A third angel followed them and said in a loud voice: "If anyone worships the beast and his image and receives his mark on the forehead or on the hand, he, too, will drink of the wine of God's fury, which has been poured full strength into the cup of his wrath. He will be tormented with burning sulfur in the presence of the holy angels and of the Lamb. And the smoke of their torment rises for ever and ever. There is no rest day or night for those who worship the beast and his image, or for anyone who receives the mark of his name." This calls for patient endurance on the part of the saints who obey God's commandments and remain faithful to Jesus.[173]

119
Seven Angels, Seven Plagues

I saw in heaven another great and marvelous sign: seven angels with the seven last plagues—last, because with them God's wrath is completed. And I saw what looked like a sea of glass mixed with fire and, standing beside the sea, those who had been victorious over the beast and his image and over the number of his name. They held harps given them by God and sang the song of Moses the servant of God and the song of the Lamb: "Great and marvelous are your deeds, Lord God Almighty. Just and true are your ways, King of the ages. Who will not fear you, O Lord, and bring glory to your name? For you alone are holy. All nations will come and worship before you, for your righteous acts have been revealed."

After this I looked and in heaven the temple was opened. Out of the temple came the seven angels with the seven plagues. They were dressed in clean, shining linen and wore golden sashes around their chests. Then one of the four living creatures gave to the seven angels seven golden bowls filled with the wrath of God, who lives for ever and ever. And the temple was filled with smoke from the glory of God and from his power, and no one could enter the temple until the seven plagues of the seven angels were completed.[174]

120

Dazed by the Heavenly Court

Suddenly I felt my brow forced down
by light far brighter than I sensed before;
my mind was stunned by what it did not know.

I placed both of my hands above my eyes
and used them as a visor for my face
to temper the intensity of light.

"Dear father, what is this? There is no way
for me to shield my eyes from such bright light;
it's moving toward us, isn't it?" I asked.

"Don't be surprised if you can still be dazed
by members of the Heavenly Court," he said.
"This is our invitation to ascend.

"Not long from now, a sight like this will prove
to be no burden, but a joy as great
as Nature has prepared your soul to feel."

Before the blessed angel now we stood.
He joyfully announced: "Enter this way
to stairs less steep by far than those below."

Past him we went, already climbing when
Beati misericordes from behind
came ringing, and "Conqueror, rejoice."[175]

121
Worthy Is the Lamb!

All hail the pow'r of Jesus' name!
Let angels prostrate fall;
Bring forth the royal diadem,
And crown him Lord of all![176]

∞

The good angels hold cheap all that knowledge of material and transitory things which the demons are so proud of possessing—not that they are ignorant of these things, but because the love of God, whereby they are sanctified, is very dear to them, and because, in comparison of that not merely immaterial but also unchangeable and ineffable beauty, with the holy love of which they are inflamed, they despise all things which are beneath it and all that is not it, that they may with every good thing that is in them enjoy that good which is the source of their goodness.[177]

∞

Then I looked and heard the voice of many angels, numbering thousands upon thousands, and ten thousand times ten thousand. They encircled the throne and the living creatures and the elders. In a loud voice they sang: "Worthy is the Lamb, who was slain, to receive power and wealth and wisdom and strength and honor and glory and praise!"

Then I heard every creature in heaven and on earth and under the earth and on the sea, and all that is in them, singing: "To him who sits on the throne and to the Lamb be praise and honor and glory and power, for ever and ever!" The four living creatures said, "Amen," and the elders fell down and worshiped.[178]

∞

NOTES

1. Billy Graham, *Angels: God's Secret Agents* (Waco, Tex.: Word, 1975), 129.
2. Ann Spangler, *An Angel a Day* (Grand Rapids, Mich.: Zondervan, 1994), 21-22.
3. David Connolly, *In Search of Angels* (New York: Putnam, 1993), 26.
4. Charlie W. Shedd, *Brush of an Angel's Wing* (Ann Arbor, Mich.: Servant, 1994), 53.
5. Graham, 26-27.
6. Gary Kinnaman, *Angels Dark and Light* (Ann Arbor, Mich.: Servant, 1994), 85.
7. Graham, 24.
8. Daniel 3:10-20, 22-25, 28, NIV.
9. Dorothy Donnelly, *God and the Apple of His Eye* (Libertyville, Ill.: Prow Books/Franciscan Marytown Press, 1973), 96.
10. Jill Haak Adels, *The Wisdom of the Saints* (New York: Oxford University Press, 1987), 22.
11. James Pruitt, *Angels Beside You* (New York: Avon, 1994), 14.
12. Spangler, 12-13.
13. *His Mysterious Ways,* compiled by the editors of Guideposts (Carmel, N.Y.: Guideposts Associates, 1988), 167.
14. Composite of various sources.
15. Acts 27:15-18, 20-25, NIV.
16. Brad Steiger and Sherry Hansen Steiger, *Angels over Their Shoulders* (New York: Ballantine, 1995), 8-9.
17. Matthew 18:10, NIV.
18. Spangler, 16.
19. Rex Warner, trans., *The Confessions of St. Augustine* (New York: The New American Library, 1963), 295, 291.
20. Eileen Elias Freeman, *Touched by Angels* (New York: Warner, 1993), 54.

21. Mary Drahos, *Angels of God, Our Guardians Dear* (Ann Arbor, Mich.: Servant, 1995), 32.

22. Drahos, 21.

23. Graham, 53.

24. Revelation 4:5-11, NIV.

25. Mark Musa, trans., *Dante's Purgatory* (Bloomington, Ind.: Indiana University Press, 1981), 261.

26. Revelation 22:8-9, NIV.

27. St. Augustine, *The City of God*, Book X, Chapter 2; from *Great Books of the Western World*, Vol. 18 (Chicago: Encyclopedia Brittanica, 1952).

28. St. Augustine, *The City of God*, Book X, Chapter 3.

29. Drahos, 156.

30. Drahos, 68.

31. St. Augustine, *The City of God*, Book X, Chapter 1.

32. "Angel Voices, Ever Singing." Text: Francis Pott; Music: Arthur S. Sullivan.

33. Spangler, 183.

34. Drahos, 15657.

35. Steiger, 13-14.

36. Marilynn Carlson Webber and William D. Webber, *A Rustle of Angels* (Grand Rapids, Mich.: Zondervan, 1994), 49-50.

37. "Angels Watchin' Over Me," American spiritual.

38. Connolly, 26.

39. Graham, 75-76.

40. Basilea Schlink, *The Unseen World of Angels and Demons* (Old Tappan, N.J.: Chosen, 1986) 137, as retold in *Where Angels Walk,* by Joan Wester Anderson (Huntington, N.Y.: Barton & Brett, 1992), 148-49. Reprinted with permission.

41. Anderson, 147-48.

42. Shedd, 24-26.

43. Steiger, 31-32.

44. Webber, 45-46.

45. Charlie W. Shedd, *What Children Tell Me about Angels* (Ann Arbor, Mich.: Servant, 1995), 31-32.

46. Kinnaman, 60.
47. 1 John 1:5b, *The Message*.
48. 1 Peter 3:22, NIV.
49. Acts 10:1-8, 17-18, 21-23, NIV.
50. Freeman, 17273.
51. Freeman, 55.
52. St. Augustine, *The City of God*, Book X, Chapter 7.
53. Jewish Prayer from the *Siddur*, as quoted in Morris B. Margolies, *A Gathering of Angels* (New York: Ballantine, 1994), 224.
54. "O Come, All Ye Faithful." Latin hymn, ascribed to John Francis Wade.
55. Psalms 103:20, NIV.
56. As quoted in Connolly, 30.
57. Emanuel Swedenborg, as quoted in Samuel M. Warren, *A Compendium of the Theological Writings of Emanuel Swedenborg* (New York: Swedenborg Foundation, 1875), 664.
58. Revelation 19:1-7, 9, NIV.
59. Freeman, 28-29.
60. Webber, 171.
61. Mark Rutland, *Behind the Glittering Mask* (Ann Arbor, Mich.: Servant, 1996), 163-64.
62. Amelia Earhart, as quoted in Lee Ann Chearney, ed., *The Quotable Angel* (New York: John Wiley & Sons, 1995), 78.
63. Excerpted from "The Kingdom of God," by Francis Thompson (1859-1907).
64. Bert Ghezzi, adapted from *Miracles of the Saints* (Grand Rapids, Mich.: Zondervan, 1996).
65. Andrew J. Bandstra, *In the Company of Angels* (Ann Arbor, Mich.: Servant, 1995), 25-26.
66. *His Mysterious Ways*, 65-66.
67. Hebrews 13:2, NIV.
68. Kathryn Deering. Used by permission.
69. Thomas Hobbes, *Leviathan* (Oxford: Basil Blackwell, 1957), Part 3, Chapter 34.

70. Revelation 22:1-6, *The Message*.
71. Hebrews 1:13-14, NIV.
72. Genesis 16:7-13, NIV.
73. Luke 1:5-9, 11-15, 17-19, NIV.
74. 1 Kings 19:1-8, NIV.
75. Genesis 28:10-18, LB.
76. Spangler, 185.
77. Daniel 6:6-12, 16, 19-23, NIV.
78. Luke 1:26-38, NIV.
79. "It Came Upon the Midnight Clear." Text: Edmund H. Sears; Music: Richard S. Willis.
80. C. S. Lewis, as quoted in Chearney, 28.
81. Luke 2:8-15, *The Message*.
82. "Hark! the Herald Angels Sing." Text: Charles Wesley; Music: Felix Mendelssohn.
83. Spangler, 66-67.
84. "While Shepherds Watched Their Flocks." Text: Nahum Tate; Music: George F. Handel.
85. "Angels, from the Realms of Glory." Text: James Montgomery; Music: Henry Smart.
86. Spangler, 91-92.
87. Graham, 36-37.
88. Ezekiel 28:12-19, LB.
89. Ezekiel 1:22-24, NIV.
90. William Shakespeare, as quoted in Chearney, 80.
91. Revelation 18:1, NIV.
92. Ezekiel 1:4-14, LB.
93. Kinnaman, 54.
94. Drahos, 29-30.
95. Matthew 28:2-3, NIV.
96. Musa, 82-83.
97. Freeman, 85-86.
98. Musa, 13031.

99. Based on Malcolm Muggeridge, *Something Beautiful for God* (New York, Harper & Row, 1971), 43-44.

100. Joshua 5:13-15, LB.

101. Shedd, *What Children Tell Me about Angels,* 14445.

102. Shedd, *What Children Tell Me about Angels,* 90-92.

103. Exodus 23:30; 13:21-22, NIV.

104. Kathryn Deering. Used by permission.

105. Genesis 18:2-8, NIV; Genesis 19:1-3, NIV.

106. Revelation 10:1-4, 8-10, LB.

107. 2 Kings 6:15-17, LB.

108. Kinnaman, 96.

109. Psalms 91:11-12, *The Message.*

110. Psalms 34:6-7, *The Message.*

111. Psalms 35:4b-6, *The Message.*

112. Numbers 22:23-27, 31-32, NIV.

113. Spangler, 37-38.

114. Nathaniel Hawthorne, as quoted in Chearney, 96.

115. Freeman, 41.

116. Emily Dickinson, as quoted in Chearney, 22.

117. Judges 13:2-6, 8-11, 12-13, 15-20, LB.

118. Corrie ten Boom, *Marching Orders for the End of Battle* (Fort Washington, Pa.: Christian Literature Crusade, 1969), 89-90, as retold in Anderson, 146.

119. Musa, 17-18.

120. 2 Chronicles 32:16-22, LB.

121. Acts 12:23, NIV.

122. Acts 5:17-21, NIV.

123. Graham, 37.

124. St. Thomas Aquinas, as quoted in Chearney, 51.

125. Drahos, 76.

126. Musa, 182-83.

127. Webber, 25.

128. Anderson, 88-89.

129. Anderson, 71-73.

130. *His Mysterious Ways*, 16-17.

131. Omer Englebert, *St. Francis of Assisi: A Biography* (Ann Arbor, Mich.: Servant, 1979), 257-58.

132. Peter Kreeft, *The Angel and the Ants* (Ann Arbor, Mich.: Servant, 1994) 139-42.

133. Esther de Waal, *Every Earthly Blessing* (Ann Arbor, Mich.: Servant, 1991) 11, 19-20.

134. Webber, 24.

135. Drahos, 43-44.

136. Anderson, 89-90.

137. Freeman, 69.

138. Bandstra, 126.

139. Kinnaman, 105-106.

140. Spangler, 156-57.

141. Graham, 113-14.

142. Kinnaman, 101.

143. Matthew 28:1-10, *The Message*.

144. Graham, 116.

145. Drahos, 168-169.

146. Spangler, 154-55.

147. Steiger, 178-79.

148. Kinnaman, 88-89.

149. 2 Corinthians 11:14, NIV.

150. Mortimer J. Adler and William Gorman, eds., *A Syntopicon of Great Books of the Western World*, (Chicago: Encyclopedia Britannica, 1952), 8.

151. St. Augustine, *The City of God*, Book XII, Chapter 1 (New York: Random House, 1950), 380.

152. St. Augustine, *The City of God*, Book XII, Chapter 6.

153. John Freccero, *Dante: The Poetics of Conversion* (Cambridge, Mass.: Harvard University Press, 1986), 110.

154. Miguel De Unamuno, as quoted in Chearney, 104.

155. Billy Graham, as quoted in Chearney, 95.

156. Revelation 20:1-3, NIV.
157. Graham, 30.
158. Numbers 20:16, NIV.
159. Graham, 23.
160. Graham, 34.
161. Genesis 22:9-13, 15-18, NIV.
162. 1 Chronicles 21:15-18, 26-27, NIV.
163. Matthew 4:1-11, NIV.
164. Spangler, 135-37.
165. St. Augustine, *The City of God*, Book IX, Chap. 21.
166. Musa, 129.
167. Revelation 12:7-12, NIV.
168. Anne Field, *The Binding of the Strong Man: The Teaching of St. Leo the Great* (Ann Arbor, Mich.: Word of Life, 1976), 98.
169. Bandstra, 81-82.
170. Graham, 81-82.
171. Matthew 24:30-31; 25:31-34, 41, NIV.
172. Matthew 13:36-43, 47-50, NIV.
173. Revelation 14:6-12, NIV.
174. Revelation 15:1-8, NIV.
175. Musa, 161-62.
176. "All Hail the Power of Jesus' Name." Text: Edward Perronet; Music: Oliver Holden.
177. St. Augustine, *The City of God,* Book IX, Chapter 22.
178. Revelation 5:11-14, NIV.

ACKNOWLEDGMENTS

Excerpts from *Angels Over Their Shoulders,* by Brad Steiger and Sherry Hansen Steiger, © 1995 by Brad Steiger and Sherry Hansen Steiger, reprinted by permission of Ballantine Books, a division of Random House, Inc.

Excerpts from *Where Angels Walk: True Stories of Heavenly Visitors,* by Joan Wester Anderson, © 1992 by Joan Wester Anderson, published by Barton & Brett, Publishers, Inc., Huntington, N.Y., reprinted by permission.

Excerpts from *Confessions* and from *The City of God,* by St. Augustine of Hippo, reprinted with permission from *Great Books of the Western World,* © 1952, 1990 Encyclopedia Britannica, Inc.

Excerpts from *His Mysterious Ways,* compiled by the editors of Guideposts, © 1988: Excerpt by Mary Hattan Bogart, from August 1988 issue of Guideposts Magazine, reprinted by permission of author. Excerpt by Euphie Eallonardo adapted with permission from Guideposts Magazine, © 1982 by Guideposts, Carmel, N.Y. 10512. Excerpt by Sylvia W. Stevens adapted with permission of Guideposts Magazine, © 1984 by Guideposts, Carmel, N.Y. 10512.

Excerpts from *Dante's Purgatory,* translated by Mark Musa, © 1981, reprinted by permission of Indiana University Press.

Excerpts from the following reprinted by permission of Servant Publications, Ann Arbor, Mich.: *What Children Tell Me About Angels,* by Charlie Shedd, © 1995; *Angels Dark and Light,* by Gary Kinnaman, © 1994; and *Angels of God, Our Guardians Dear,* by Mary Drahos, © 1995.

Excerpts from *Touched by Angels,* by Eileen Elias Freeman, reprinted by permission of Warner Books, Inc., New York, N.Y., U.S.A. © 1993 by Eileen Elias Freeman. All rights reserved.